The Motorhome…
what you need to know, before you go.

Also by Ali Kingston
E-book: **Motorhome Life... A Few Tips and Ideas**

Reader Reviews for Motorhome Life... A Few Tips and Ideas

*'I found this really informative and very easy to read, with lots of tips!
Looking forward to reading Ali's next book'*
October 2014

*'Lots of useful advice for anyone planning a holiday or longer in a
motorhome (or caravan). When the day comes when we no longer have
commitments at home (farm and lots of pets!), I hope we can pack up lightly
and go out to explore'*
September 2014

*'Excellent Read. I'm on the verge of becoming a full timer and this book has
provided excellent hints and tips into this and provided an insight into Ali
and Mike's life on the road'*
August 2014

*'Very Useful. I love this book and there is a wealth of information in it.
It's easy to read and very helpful. We met Ali and Mike in Morocco some years
ago when we were full timing too. Their advice, friendship and generosity stood
us in good stead for our future travels. I have followed Mike's example and
dumped the hosepipe. I now use a watering can too. It's actually so much easier.
I would heartily recommend this book to anyone who was thinking of going
travelling in a motorhome. The websites referred to are the ones we use regularly
ourselves and even the experienced full-timers will probably find some useful bits
in it, I know I did'*
July 2014

'A must for anyone thinking of holidaying in/purchasing a home on wheels. All these tips for less than the price of a coffee? I was recommended this book by a friend, as my husband and I are thinking of purchasing a motorhome. So I picked it up and thought "I suppose I had better read it", and to be honest, I thought it would be a chore. How wrong was I! I could not put this book down. It is full of very handy, useful, everyday tips, and gives a little insight into Ali and Mike's life in their home on wheels. A must for anybody who is either thinking of going on holiday in or purchasing a motorhome. It has given us a true record of what to expect, is full of motorhoming terms, and wonderful, personal photographs. Well done to the author for producing such a great book.'
July 2014

'I'd been thinking about living in a motor home for a while and wanted first-hand information on it. This book is comprehensive; organised and exactly what I wanted to read. Ali's personal anecdotes bring it all to life. If you are considering this way of life, Ali's checklist will force you to think about some things that perhaps you hadn't before'
July 2014.

'Prospective motorhome owners or full-timers should start here! For every person living full time in their motorhome there must be hundreds who would like to do the same or are about to take the plunge. This book is packed full of useful information on what to look for when buying a motorhome and how to get the best out of it. Peppered throughout the book are tips and anecdotes from Ali and Mike's extensive travels in Europe and the US. They have been living full time in their motorhome since way back in 2002 so you can be sure they know a thing or two about the subject. Anyone thinking about buying a motorhome and maybe leaving the rat race behind will find this book very useful.'
June 2014

The Motorhome…
what you need to know, before you go.

by **Ali Kingston**

Motorhome Lifer Publishing
November 2014

Published by Motorhome Lifer Publishing 2014
Text and Images ©2014 Ali Kingston
All Rights Reserved

A CIP catalogue record for this book is available from the British Library.

ISBN 978-0-9929612-4-4

Front cover design Neil Tweddle

For Mike

Contents

Introduction

Preface

In 2012 I published a website with practical tips and advice for anyone interested in our lifestyle. When I set it up, I called it Motorhome Lifers. My aim was to give it a catchy name that would convey what we do. I also chose it because for some, this way of life could feel like a prison sentence. Not to give a direct comparison with prison life but that one man's meat is another man's poison.

This book presents the pages from the website in a more structured way. I have included everything I can think of, based on our experiences to date, but it's not exhaustive. My aim has been to give a flavour of our world and address many questions that people ask us.

Ali Kingston
November 2014

Introduction

Chapter One – I explain the types of motorhome and how to choose one to fit your needs. You have worked hard to be able to afford this expensive investment and don't want regrets if you have made the wrong decision.

Chapter Two – Information for everyday living. This chapter covers aspects of life we take for granted at home, such as how to obtain fresh water, deal with waste and cope with temperature fluctuations. Utilities, such as water, electricity and gas can be a limited resource when you're away.

Chapter Three – Safety and security issues. It's not all doom and gloom but you need to be aware of some hazards and pitfalls. Learn how not to become a victim of an opportunistic crime.

Chapter Four – Save time while you're away with guidance on where to stay and how to find suitable stop-over spots.

Chapter Five – You may have planned to 'live the dream' for many years, but not spent extended periods of time up close and personal with your life partner. Gain insight into relationship management on the road.

Chapter Six – How do you know how much it all costs to live full-time in a motorhome? To help point you in the right direction find out how we work out the finances.

Chapter Seven – Keeping in touch with loved ones on a long trip away is a necessity. Loneliness could become a real issue and I share some communication methods.

Chapter Eight – A few tips if going beyond European borders.

There are over 90 web links provided at the end of the book to assist you with further research.

When we set off on our first adventure, we chucked what we thought we needed into the back of our new motorhome and set off, then we learnt through experience. I have written this book to help fellow motorhomers on their journey. At times our learning curve was steep, and by sharing some of our anecdotes, I hope you can avoid some mishaps. Please bear in mind that the information doesn't constitute advice and is given for guidance and in good faith.

This book may mark a new beginning, or could put you off motorhomes entirely and save you a considerable amount of expense and heartache. Then you can get on with life and enjoy your home comforts. Who knows how you will feel? This will give you an idea, so what are you waiting for? Put your feet up and get reading. This is a window into our world.

Chapter One
Choosing a Motorhome

I recently met a young couple on a campsite who had borrowed their friends' campervan. I was struck by how thrilled they were with their overnight accommodation. The owner had thoughtfully stocked the cupboards with snacks, treats and a bottle of bubbly, which must have enhanced the sense of occasion but their response to their campervan almost had a childlike air of innocence. They couldn't believe that everything they needed was with them, or that it was so warm, dry and comfortable compared to a tent, which was what they were used to. On the flip-side I have also chatted to those who find our nomadic ways confusing because they cannot believe anyone in their right minds would even consider living in a metal box.

If the delighted couple went on to choose a motorhome they would probably find it all quite bewildering, as there are several types available with endless styles, shapes and sizes to suit all tastes and budgets. Once you know some of the jargon and identify what your needs are, making a choice becomes easier.

When we bought our first motorhome, my husband Mike made the decision on what would be best for us. He had owned a caravan when his children were young, and although they aren't exactly the same, there are many similarities, so I thought he was well qualified. When he did the research my only stipulation was that I didn't want to be cold while we were away. My ideal winter would be to crawl into a nice warm airing cupboard at the end of October. It would be stocked with clean, fresh smelling laundry and I could sleep there until the beginning of March when I would be ready to return to the real world for the spring. Clearly, this fantasy is unattainable and a solution is to head for a milder climate during these months. What better way than with mobile accommodation?

The spell checker underlines motorhome in angry red, as though motor and home shouldn't be combined into one word. As it provides a little home on wheels, I think they go together perfectly.

There aren't many words for motorhome. I looked up the DVLA (Driver

Vehicle Licensing Agency) definition and found that they refer to one as motor caravan, motorhome, campervan and camper van. In magazines and reference books you may notice this abbreviated to 'van. The apostrophe denotes the missing 'cara' before van. This ensures that the reader doesn't get confused with commercial vans. I have seen the abbreviation 'moho' used, which has a catchy ring to it and makes a change from formal sounding terms.

Owners often christen their vehicle. Our friends, Jon and Linda, have a car, tandem and motorhome and each one has a name. When our motorhome was new they challenged us to choose a name, but how could we come up with anything as good as Tilly, Taffy or Pumpkin?

The colour of our current van is listed as Pearlescent Grey by Citroen. This must be a naughty fifty-first shade of grey because the spell checker picks up on Pearlescent as well. Anyway, I shortened it and created the girl's name, Pearl. However, the only people who call her Pearl are Jon and Linda and we still refer to her as the van or the motorhome.

A photograph of Pearl is on the opposite page, she is sunning herself on a cliff top in Portugal during her first winter.

Coachbuilt Motorhome

The living accommodation on this type of motorhome is bonded onto the chassis of the vehicle and this is done at a separate manufacturing facility. In Europe the engine suppliers include Ford, Fiat, Peugeot, Citroen, MAN, Iveco, Volkswagen and Mercedes.

There are many different configurations for the layout of the living area. There may be bunk beds for children, a garage to store a scooter or a car. We once saw one at the Düsseldorf Show in Germany with a built in sauna.

'A' Class Motorhome

The motorhome is built around the chassis, which is integral to the vehicle and so you don't see a separate cab. Some of these are big and look like a coach from the outside. If you can afford one of the large ones you must have the funds to maintain and run it. Spare parts, servicing and maintenance are all more expensive and because they have a big powerful engine they use a lot of fuel. Most European companies manufacture a full range of motorhomes.

You may see American 'A' Class motorhomes, imported from the USA and registered in Britain when they arrive. When we owned an American 'A' Class our consumption was 10-12 mpg (miles per gallon), but the European manufacturers advertise the new ones at 18-24 mpg.

An American motorhome is sometimes referred to as a Winnebago. This is a trade name that has become generic, similar to a Hoover which should correctly be called a vacuum cleaner, but we generally refer to one as a hoover. If you are interested in an RV there is a whole new dictionary of terms to become acquainted with.

Careful research needs to be done before purchasing an RV because some are illegal to drive on British roads. They may be too wide and you also need to check with DVLA if you require a Heavy Goods Vehicle (HGV) Licence to drive one. Mike's licence entitles him to drive a vehicle up to 7500kg.

Other Types of Vehicle

Once you're interested in a motorhome, they seem to crop up all over. Here are some varieties; bespoke conversions such as SC Sporthomes, converted buses, trucks, vans, all-terrain vehicles such as Unimog with living accommodation, classics such as the VW transporter, day vans, and mini campers, such as Romahome, or the Wildax Cutie.

What Were We Thinking?

Mike took a year out in 1996 to travel around the world. This belated gap year gave him wanderlust and when he got back he realised that he wanted to live on the move. Soon after we met in 2000, we went on a seven week backpacking trip to India. Having survived and enjoyed those rigours we were soon planning an 'alternative' lifestyle which would combine living and travelling.

We considered a houseboat and a longboat but towards the end of 2001, while on holiday in Garruchia in Spain, we noticed an almost constant stream of motorhomes trundling along the coast road, in view of our hotel balcony. We learned that they were from northern Europe and heading south for the winter. They were the human equivalent of snow birds. On our return from this holiday Mike's research went into overdrive and as a result we purchased our first motorhome a few months later.

Each of our choices has been made with the intention of providing us with a home. Our first motorhome was a good option for full-time living. She was sometimes oversized for bridges, roads, campsites and car parks but we were generally able to get around without difficulty.

We shipped her to the States for our second year and took our belongings with us. You may be wondering why we would want to go to such inconvenience when there are so many other ways to tour America. These include fly-drive, renting a motorhome or buying a Recreational Vehicle (American term for motorhome). Mike had read an article in a magazine, written by a couple who shipped their motorhome across on a Temporary Import Bond. If they could do it, why not us? Renting was expensive but the cost of shipping, spread over a twelve month period made it affordable. (Less than £3500 for the round trip.) To give you an idea, at today's prices, one month RV (Recreational Vehicle) rental in Florida during November 2014 would set you back $2670 or £1589 at the exchange rate during June 2014. This doesn't include campground fees or tax.

The idea of taking our European motorhome appealed to me because this would be an unconventional way of making the trip.

While we were in America, other drivers would like to comment on what to them was a very strange looking vehicle, and far too small to live in full-time. On one occasion, after a fuel fill-up in California, another customer shouted across the forecourt;

"Hey guys, you're brave bringing that thing over here. In my day Fiat stood for 'Fix It Again Tony'"

Many Americans live year round in their motorhome and they have large vehicles that provide a true home from home with full sized domestic fixtures and fittings. These mobile homes on wheels are known as recreational vehicles and this is abbreviated to RV. While we toured the States we thought this set up would suit us and when we got back we traded the CI for a Forest River Sunseeker. This was a 'C' Class American motorhome.

We have been asked with the benefit of hindsight if we feel it was a mistake to ship our European motorhome to America, only to buy an American one in the UK on our return. On reflection, it would have made more sense to sell our British motorhome, then buy another in the States to tour in and then ship it back afterwards. However, this didn't occur to us at the time, we wanted to go on a US road trip and because our motorhome had been our home for a year, she was fully kitted out, reliable and as you will learn later, Mike was in love with her. Yes, really.

In 2008 we purchased an 'A' Class RV in Florida. Our plan was to tour the USA for regular six month stints, but unfortunately she proved so unreliable that we were forced to sell after only eight months.

After we sold the 'A' Class in America, we decided to downsize and return to a vehicle designed for the smaller roads of Europe. After careful consideration we chose a van conversion. This has given us freedom and flexibility with the ability to park virtually anywhere.

The Homes in More Detail

Our first motorhome met all our needs for a couple wanting to live this way full-time. It was also big enough to have friends and family to stay. The model was a CI (Caravans International) Riviera 181, on a Fiat Chassis and 7m long (approximately 23ft). At the time we bought it the dealer and the manufacturer classified it as a 'C' Class. Nowadays the term coachbuilt is more commonly used, although some dealers still advertise this type as 'C' Class. No wonder motorhomes can be confusing!

The CI had a double bed above the cab, which we slept in, and to get there we climbed a ladder; a bit like getting onto the top of a bunk bed. A permanent bed saved us from having to reconstruct and remake it at night. Two long seats faced each other on the sides at the rear, with another across the back to form a 'U' shaped seat. On the other side was a wide shelf, about the size of the top of a single kitchen unit, which provided a useful surface for our portable television when we were ready to watch it. It wasn't sophisticated enough to enable tuning in to European channels. We wouldn't have understood them anyway, but all we could watch was 'The World at War Series', a huge video box set, that Mike had been given for Christmas and that was all we had. In the evenings of our first trip away we would sit down and watch another episode, or even two. Although it was informative I found the history harrowing and would have preferred to watch something more light-hearted. The series has been advertised on TV recently. As soon as I heard the background music again I was transported straight back to that first trip and felt relieved that we have so much more choice nowadays. Isn't it strange how memories come back?

Modern motorhomes usually have a flat screen TV, fixed with a bracket. Some are built into a cupboard and stored out of sight.

The next photo is of our motorhome at a campground in the Mojave Desert, California. You can see the extended space over the cab which gives a slightly domed appearance from the outside.

In the mid-section of the van there was a bathroom with shower and toilet together. Opposite this was the kitchen area, complete with a cooker, comprising of a gas oven, grill and hob. Underneath the sink, a fridge. Directly behind the cab on the passenger side was a dinette which consisted of two double seats facing each other and a table in between; a bit like a train but with pretty upholstery. Across the corridor from this was the door to the outside. The cab was the same as a commercial van and had a curtain to divide it from the living area, which gave privacy and a more homely feel when we closed it at night. This was a six berth motorhome because the dinette table and chairs, as well as the seating area at the back could be converted into a double bed.

The driver and passenger seats in the cab were fixed and permanently faced forwards. Most new motorhomes these days are manufactured so that these seats swivel to face the rear when the vehicle is parked. This increases the living space and provides two extra chairs.

Not long after our return from the States we visited the Motorhome and Caravan Show at the National Exhibition Centre (NEC) in Birmingham. The night before the show I found Mike flicking through brochures and magazine articles with features on large European motorhomes. He asked me what I thought about these vehicles. I couldn't give a definite answer, but I liked our CI and thought the pictures of the ones he was perusing looked amazing, but really expensive.

When we arrived at the NEC, an American 'C' Class RV seemed to block the entrance of the exhibition hall and we practically bumped into it when we arrived. It had been imported to the UK by the dealership and they had undertaken the necessary modifications for Europe. This included a transformer to convert our UK 240v electricity supply down to 110v that the fitted appliances ran on inside the RV. British three pin sockets had been fitted where the original American ones had been.

When I stepped up inside the living area I was struck by how light and spacious it was inside. This was because the ceiling was higher than I was used to and it had a slide-out. This is a modification, where part of the side of the van is moved outwards and operated by a switch inside the vehicle. This made the main living area approximately a third wider, therefore roomier inside. There was space for a double bed over the cab, but this had been converted into what the manufacturer described as an entertainment centre. There was a glass fronted cabinet either side of a flat screen television.

The photograph overleaf shows the main living area. You can see that the slide is out because of the relative width compared to the position of the driver's seat. On the right hand side of the picture, in the kitchen, were full sized domestic appliances, including fridge-freezer, gas cooker and above this, a microwave oven.

Facing the rear, beyond the dining area, was a domestic size shower cubicle. It was on the left of the corridor and had a separate toilet opposite this. Mike was impressed with the toilet because it was a 'proper' flushing, porcelain type. At the very back was a bedroom with a queen sized bed. There was enough space to walk around this, and there was a small cupboard on each side of it.

Having looked around this motorhome first, the others at the show seemed poky in comparison, even the large luxury 'A' Classes manufactured in Europe, because none of them had the extra width created by the slide out. The Sunseeker had tasteful upholstery and décor but the European ones had a more stylish finish.

We returned to the stand several times, asking more questions on each visit. I was beginning to imagine living in it, and the way the conversations were going between Mike and the salesman this was a possibility. Soon serious negotiations were under way and the dealer agreed to include in the asking price, all the extras, including long-range liquid propane (LPG) fuel tanks, the entertainment centre and a solar panel.

Ever since we'd seen RVs during our America trip, Mike had been unable to get the idea of owning one out of his mind. He said that this was because of the extra space for full time living but I have a suspicion that it could have been more to do with the flushing porcelain toilet. All joking apart, Mike wasn't making a snap decision, although it seemed that way at the time. We bought the RV that day and agreed to trade in the CI as part of the deal.

I felt sad saying goodbye to our first motorhome. She had taken us many miles and given us so much enjoyment. She meant more to me than a vehicle or a house, and I felt a similar pull towards her as I had towards my first car.

I had an emotional bond with the CI, Mike's feelings had gone to dizzy heights, and I wasn't alone in teasing him about how he cherished her. There had been clues from the early days; the way his eyes misted over and pupils dilated when she was mentioned; his constant admiration of her sleek Italian lines and engine. She'd never disappointed him by breaking down, and the trip to America was based in large part on her sound engineering and dependability. He held the kind of tenderness and respect for her that meant that a molecule of sauce on a seat cover, globule of gravy on the carpet, or droplet of wine cascading off a chin towards the floor would have him dashing for cleaning fluid, admonishing the sloppy bon vivant in the process. If I had the misfortune of bumping my head on a door frame for example, this would manifest itself into his grave concern, not for my physical well-being but that I hadn't dented, damaged or hurt his darling.

However, her time was up, Mike transferred his affections to our new vehicle and we soon adjusted to a new way of life.

When we lived in the Sunseeker, we usually spent approximately six weeks at each spot. I thought each relocation was equivalent to a mini house move. It took a day to pack up our kit which included, amongst other bits and pieces; a tent, (which could also be used as an awning), windbreak, groundsheet, satellite dish and an external gas cylinder.

We usually did a full day's drive to get us to a new region. Manoeuvring was difficult because many European roads are narrow, even the toll booths on motorways provided a challenging squeeze.

We always pre-booked our next campsite and made it clear that we had an oversized vehicle. Often we were welcomed with glee on the telephone, but when we arrived, it transpired that they didn't have the space. On one occasion we were literally shooed off the premises when the owner saw how big we were and he completely denied taking the booking.

Trying to get on to a pitch would be difficult as our progress on site would be hampered by low entrances, overhanging trees, narrow lanes, and small pitches. Once we had found a suitable spot, and if we were planning on staying more than a few days at our new locale, all our gear had to be unpacked and set up again. However, once organised, we had a home from home and it was possible to have guests and entertain, which we both enjoyed.

We used motorways and travelled on a Sunday. The traffic was much lighter because most trucks are prohibited from driving in mainland Europe at weekends.

I found my duties as navigator onerous. You can see from the photographs how big the motorhome was; it was over 31ft long and with the car in tow the combined length was approximately 46ft, giving additional practical problems. If we missed a turn we couldn't reverse because the front wheels of the car locked if we attempted to do so. This also meant that three point turns were out of the question. We usually had to keep driving until the next roundabout, where we could go back the way we had come because it would be unusual to find a big enough space for a 'U' turn. We often ended up unhitching the car and turning each vehicle around separately. Even then the Sunseeker had a poor turning circle, unlike the CI which pirouetted on a penny.

Driving this monster was tough on Mike, but I found the pressure not to make a map reading error intense. An unspoken, undocumented law seemed to dictate that as we turned down a narrow lane, with no room to pass, a huge truck would come towards us.

Our motorhome is our home and this is a way of life for us, not a retirement package, gap year or break. Therefore, it may sound indulgent, but we do take holidays from the van.

We had been living in the Sunseeker for eighteen months, when in 2008 we went to Florida to stay with friends. As we drove our hire car from the airport to their house we noticed hoardings advertising Lazydays. This is an RV dealership that we had heard of from other owners for a couple of reasons. One was that they stocked spares for our motorhome back in Europe, at much lower prices; the other is that Lazydays is no ordinary dealership. They sell over 8000 units a year making it the largest dealership in the world. Having seen the signs we couldn't drive past without stopping and it wasn't long before we were looking inside motorhomes on display. Golf carts were provided to get around the 130 acre area and we were left in peace to appraise the merchandise.

It soon became clear that in America you get a lot more for your money than we do in the UK. This led us to make enquiries regarding the practicalities of owning and driving an RV in America. A member of the sales team confirmed that Mike could drive a recreational vehicle of any size and weight on his driving licence as long as we weren't getting involved in a commercial enterprise.

Mike and I enjoy travelling in America because the infrastructure is in place for road trips of all kinds, in any vehicle. The practical difficulties we face in Europe with large motorhomes are much less of an issue. There are more multi-lane highways with provision for wide vehicles. The roads over there are newer than ours, no narrow lanes lined with dry stone walls or hawthorn hedges, nor cobble stone streets to contend with.

The cost of fuel is also considerably cheaper. At the time of our visit diesel was approximately 50p a litre.

Our visas were still valid from our previous trip (more about visas in Chapter 8) and soon we were discussing the possibilities of having a second home in the USA.

Our first trip in the CI had been taken in a frenzy. Now we considered living in an RV and taking our time, like we did in Europe, but without the headaches involved getting from A to B. We would be able to live and tour over there for six months at a time, and then return to Europe where our other home would stay. We needed secure and affordable storage on each side of the Atlantic in order to make the plan work.

A few days later we went into a second RV dealership for another curiosity stop where we stumbled upon an enormous 'A' Class, in the entrance hall. This one was on special offer and so we decided to have a look inside. Our climb up the steps to the inside was rewarded with a view, not of a motorhome, but a palace.

The main living area had two slide-outs, one on each side. The one behind the driver's seat had a sofa and dining area in it. The dining area had floor to ceiling glass panels, giving a panoramic view to the outside and reminded me of a conservatory. The slide on the opposite side of this contained a fully equipped kitchen.

A flat screen television was above the front driver and passenger seats. These seats could be swivelled to face the rear when the motorhome was stationary. The bedroom was at the back and had a fitted wardrobe, a queen sized bed and two slide outs, one on each side. Between the living area and the bedroom was a domestic sized shower, across the corridor from a separate toilet with flushing (yes, porcelain), WC just like our British registered RV, and to cap it all, it was manufactured by Forest River, which I took to be a good omen.

Mike drives a hard bargain and later that holiday we purchased the motorhome. We organised a similar set up as we had in Europe with a Toyota Yaris to tow behind. We found a campsite in Florida that would store the RV for us as well as keep post on our behalf while we were away.

The first time Mike started the engine after our first week on a campsite near the dealership, it seemed as though every warning light on the dashboard illuminated, accompanied by the din of audible alarms.

This was the first in a series of false starts and hiccups. The dealership dealt with our breakdowns initially, but they soon suggested we take our continued problems up with the factory in Elkhart, Indiana, over 1200 miles north.

The manager there was empathetic and organised experts from the different component manufacturers to repair each fault under warranty. The technology seemed complicated and to give you an idea, he explained that there were four computers for engine management.

After all the repairs had been completed we set off for Alaska, believing that we could put it all behind us. We arrived in Fairbanks, Alaska via the iconic Alaskan Highway and enjoyed the celebrations for the longest day of the year.

Mike had bought a new vehicle because he didn't want to be involved with repairs or maintenance and as we had planned to leave her for long periods, reliability was a key factor.

The photograph overleaf is of our motorhome being towed off the pitch in Florida. As soon as the tow truck arrived a group of fellow campers turned up with chairs and cool boxes stocked with beer. They enjoyed the matinee but all we wanted to do was get on with our trip.

One morning, on our return south on the Alaska Highway and having spent the night on a supermarket car park in Whitehorse, the capital of the Yukon in Canada, a slide-out in the bedroom refused to retract. This was the final straw, and realising that we couldn't trust her, we made the difficult decision to sell.

Having driven 14 000 miles in America between March and August, Mike had earned a well-deserved rest from driving and we had a couple of quiet months living in the Sunseeker in Spain.

When the time came to drive her back to the UK, Tim and Nige, who Mike has been friends with since school, came out and joined him for a mini-break. I returned to England ahead of them so they could get on with a boys' adventure together.

They all enjoyed a road trip style holiday to bring her back to Britain from

Spain. I met them on their return and they all agreed that they had had a really good time, (it sounded to me like a cross between the movies Wild Hogs and RV) but they couldn't praise my abilities in navigating for Mike highly enough. My skills are appreciated by him but as we're together all the time he doesn't comment. I don't expect accolades, it's all part of the lifestyle.

Before their departure I had printed off written instructions for their route home and given some pointers on what to expect on French roads. If you have driven on the continent, you will be aware that there can be almost no warning of an impending junction. Often only one sign and the turning comes up almost immediately after it. Although they had a satnav, (satellite navigation device, GPS in the USA) maps and my directions they got lost on the Paris ring road and ended up careering towards the city centre. Nige, who is HGV trained shouted to Mike to follow a bus, even though they didn't know where it was heading for. Mike was appalled at this, but in the heat of the moment it made sense because a bus route could be trusted to be wide enough for an RV.

When Mike and I were together and he was driving, I would call out turn by turn instructions. As it was left hand drive this meant that I was on the driver's side when we were in the UK. I was in the driver's seat for overtaking, at roundabouts and pulling out of junctions.

Tim christened me the Patron Saint of Navigation but when I heard how difficult my new navigation partners found directing Mike for a single trip, my misgivings surfaced. They hadn't been towing the car with the added pressure of not being able to reverse.

The Sunseeker had a 6.8 litre, V10 Ford Triton engine and this is found in American trucks, passenger vehicles, such as mini buses, and in RVs. This large size meant that it used a lot of fuel. Mike had built this into his budget calculations and so this didn't play a part in our decision to sell, but what we had come to realise was that although our home was solid, spacious, luxurious and comfortable we were travellers at heart. We missed the flexibility to pack up and leave on a whim, because this represents freedom.

Mike, as with the first, was besotted with this motorhome but I knew he was considering selling when he said he didn't think the second hand value would justify a sale. I asked him how much in his wildest dreams he could ever hope to get for it. Fellow motorhome owners reckoned that our efforts to sell the RV in the midst of a recession would be difficult. They were convinced that no-one had the cash to purchase her, nor would they be able to afford to fund her gluttonous fuel fill ups.

She sold within 24 hrs.

Van Conversion

Our current motorhome is a van conversion that has been modified to suit our needs for full-time living. When we had a look at the vans produced by the large manufacturers we realised that we needed some extras that they would not be able to provide.

Our fourth motorhome had to meet the following criteria based on knowledge gained from our experiences up until that time:

- A fixed bed, so that we wouldn't have to construct and remake it at night.

- The large space for stores in a motorhome is often referred to as a garage. Mike could do with a vault for his baked bean harvest and although I'm no fashionista, I need a seasonal change of clothes.

- Robust high quality fixtures and fittings. A full-timing motorhome will have more wear and tear than a holidaying one.

- Solar panel, two high quality leisure batteries and several 12v sockets.

- Left-hand drive because we spend so much time in mainland Europe.

- Powerful engine and top specification on the base vehicle. Mike believes that a brand new investment deserves the best of the extras.

Mike researched independent van manufacturers and this culminated in our visit to the Wildax factory, near Huddersfield in West Yorkshire. The owner, Duncan Wildman, allowed us to sit inside one of the recently completed conversions so that we could get a better feel for what it might be like to live in.

We discussed the merits of his design at a stage whisper, out of earshot. Space was definitely limited compared with any of our previous motorhomes, but as we spend as much time as we can in sunnier climes, we thought we would mostly be outside enjoying ourselves. The freedom to be able to drive, and park where it suited us, outweighed the confines of the interior.

The layout of the Aurora Leisure would need some modifications and Duncan agreed to our requests to create a bespoke vehicle.

The original design has two long bench seats at the rear which make up into a double bed. The central part of the van contains the bathroom, kitchen and wardrobe. The front transforms into a living area; the two cab seats at the front swivel to face the rear. In this position a dinette is formed with the chairs facing the table and bench seat. A flat screen television is bracketed to the wall facing the front of the van.

The picture opposite shows the storage area above the cab with the two front seats rotated to face the living area.

To give us extra room inside and allow for an enlarged garage space underneath the bed we needed to have our motorhome built on an extra-long wheelbase. Mike chose the left-hand drive Citroen Relay (known as a Jumper on the continent). He specified a 160 HP 3 litre engine to give extra power for overtaking and additional torque for steep hills. A diesel tank of 125 litres has been fitted instead of the standard 90 litres, giving us a range of 800 miles per fill up. Wildax normally use the 5.90m wheelbase, but we had ours built on an extra, extra long 6.4m.

The living area of our van has the same layout as the original Aurora, but we have had a permanent rear bed fitted and raised off the floor to give storage underneath the bed. The bed is huge, wider than a super king size, and we sleep across the width of the van, so this design would not suit a tall person. Mike is nearly 5ft 11in. The distance from the floor to the top of the memory foam mattress is 4ft, and so we climb up to the bed using a folding stool. The extra height has given less headroom above, though this isn't a problem for us. Access is via the rear doors or from the inside, underneath the bed.

The photo below is of the garage, it looks huge but fills up too quickly.

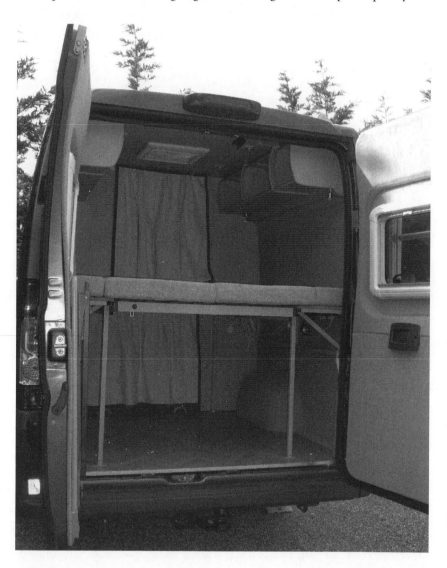

The build quality and finish of the fixtures and fittings are of a high standard and we are pleased with our choice of upholstery.

We have a 600mm x 600mm roof light, which brightens the inside and makes it feel more spacious.

I took the photo below in Novgorod, during our 2012 trip to Russia. If you look to the left, through the sliding door, you can see a tatty building. Although there are many picturesque, historic buildings to see in this World Heritage designated city, that's a derelict factory.

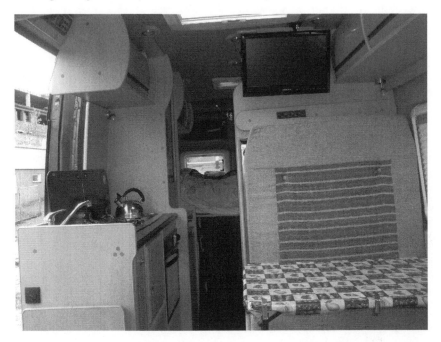

The kitchen area is well laid out and has an extra slide-out work top over the fridge which I use for chopping and slicing food and stacking dishes after washing them up. There is a two ring gas hob with an integral stainless steel sink. Below the hob is a gas cooker and grill. There is plenty of room in the cupboards for food and crockery, and a slide out pantry which has proved to be ideal for storing spices and cutlery.

We regularly exceed 32 mpg and with such good fuel consumption, long distances aren't a problem.

For our second winter in the van we decided to visit Greece and Turkey. Friends had warned us that it would be too cold but we didn't take heed of their advice. One morning during March, we woke up to snow on the beach in Turkey. Although there hadn't been any of the grey overcast days that we endure in Britain during the winter there was often a brisk, northerly wind. This meant that we had to keep our sliding door closed for long periods during the day and this made us feel cooped up. I didn't dare complain as I had been so enthusiastic about a van conversion and vociferous with my views on heading to this part of the world. However, we did learn from it and the following winter we stored the motorhome in Spain and went backpacking in Mexico.

The adjustment to living full-time with the reduced space of a van conversion probably took a couple of weeks. Only one person can be up and about doing something at any time. So, if Mike is getting dressed, I stay in bed until he is ready, or if I am cooking, he sits and watches television. Because of this I have become obsessive about putting things away as there aren't enough surfaces to leave things lying about.

If you're interested in a tailor-made vehicle, there are several small independent manufacturers dotted around the country. It's worth investing time researching on the internet and browsing through magazines.

Travellers and Dwellers

Motorhome owners can be roughly divided into two groups. These are travellers and dwellers, and you may find it useful to think about which category you fall into. (Dwellers enjoy a home from home and travellers stay on the move.) As a dweller you carry a greater load, there's more planning involved and less flexibility in terms of manoeuvrability but when you arrive at your destination you can set up for longer with all your stuff. Travellers are able to pack up quickly if they wish and make decisions on where to go based on a whim.

Storage

Because we live in a small van all year, adequate storage space is vital but there is a decision to be made, split between weight, space taken and usefulness.

We keep all our gear with us, we don't need a top box or trailer, and only our bicycles are on view at the back. There is room for folding bikes under our bed but we find full sized bikes more comfortable.

A few people choose a van conversion because the roof is suited to take the weight of a load on a roof-rack. Some vans, such as a fibre glass coachbuild are not suited for this.

My attitude towards handbags and shoes can only be described as minimalist. Our style of living has taught me that I'm a practical type and I wouldn't know where to start with fashion and designer gear. The emphasis is on hard wearing and practical. I have one hand bag - a smart leather rucksack. My dressy evening clothes may covered in sequins but they're made of 'T'-shirt fabric and roll up into a drawer. I wear my walking boots most days and have never been asked to leave a restaurant because they don't match my outfit.

Don't forget if you're constantly on the move no-one knows if you have worn the same clothes three nights in a row, and if they did, they probably wouldn't care.

There is a possibility that Mike was a squirrel in a previous life. He spends hours and hours packing, unpacking, all to make sure we have plenty of room for stores and provisions. If you see him in the right sort of weather, it's highly likely he'll be enjoying another reorganisation.

What you need in a house is different to what you use for a life on the road. When we first set out we stored what we couldn't take at an industrial unit. When we realised that our travelling was more than a transient phase, we got rid of most of it because we had what we needed. If you take a look around your home, you'll see what you have that you don't use. I bet you have loads of duplications and clutter. I found the de-junking process cathartic. We gave a lot away, involved a house clearance company, and ended up with a couple of boxes which are stored in a loft. These contain vinyl records, travel journals and photograph albums which were too important to get rid of.

Navigation

In many ways navigation has become easier with the advent of satellite navigation (satnav). If you are lost in a city it can get you out quickly. We have one and I have a bit of a love/hate relationship with it. There are several reasons for this; I like to think I know what I'm doing when it comes to map reading and I resent the voice from a machine telling us where to go. I sometimes become complacent when it's switched on and forget that a ring road or heavy goods route is more suitable for our size, rather than driving through a 3.5T restricted town centre.

One-way streets aren't always taken in to account, and you are often guided to use the most direct route, even if that's not the option you chose at start-up.

On more than one occasion we have listened to the guidance rather than using common sense. This raises our blood pressures and stresses us out. The motoring experience is much more pleasurable when you can go with the flow.

Any map, paper or electronic, won't always be up-to-date because new roads are built and routes change. If the software is designed for a car it won't take the height and width of a motorhome into account. However, if Mike is driving on his own he finds it a necessity.

When we're touring in the van Mike likes to have the satnav switched on as it gives speed limit warnings. I have a paper map on my lap for an overview.

It is worth researching these devices carefully as their specifications are changing all the time. Models designed for motorhomes are now available.

In case you're wondering, Mike drives and I navigate because if we switch roles Mike falls asleep in the passenger chair. Useless!

Additional Transport on Arrival

Initially, the CI provided our only form of transport. We walked miles and miles, which we enjoyed, but we wanted extra wheels.

While we were in Spain during our first trip, we visited a friend of ours - another Nigel. He showed us a Spartamet motorised bicycle. These are made in the Netherlands and are push-bikes with a 30cc Sachs motor fitted. They are made in traditional Dutch style, have big wheels and you sit upright to ride them. Some people say 'sit up and beg' to describe the riding position. Nigel preferred a more modern looking bike and so he had stripped the engines off a pair of original Spartamets and re-engineered mountain bikes for himself and his wife. Unfortunately, one of these had been stolen and he hadn't got round to modifying another one. He wasn't sure if he needed these bikes for himself and so he agreed to get on and adapt a second mountain bike for me while we were there. It was a complex procedure and took him three, or possibly four, full days. We bought them off him along with his repair kit, tools and panniers. They had a top speed of about 35km/hr (24mph) and turned the heads of anyone who noticed.

We would use them to go on cycle rides where walking would have taken too long. If we were in a hilly area the engine gave a fantastic boost for the climbs.

Our longest journey was from Norwich to Dereham in Norfolk, approximately 16 miles. As we both do a lot of cycling now, and are used to longer distances this doesn't sound far. (I'm now thinking it sounds like a pathetic effort, hardly worth mentioning). At the time we felt as though we had completed a major expedition with four panniers on each bike fully loaded.

Mike is keen to cycle from the UK to Portugal and thinking about it, perhaps we've got misplaced confidence in our abilities.

A few people who buy a motorhome like to tow a car behind. When we did this it was great to have a car, particularly when we were working and living in the motorhome, but this entails additional costs with tax, MOT, insurance and servicing.

When moving the complete outfit the tow vehicle may be secured to a trailer or towed four wheels down. We chose the latter option and ours had a braked 'A' frame system. Fully legal in the UK but in some European countries there have been reports of spot fines being issued by local police. I understand that there is lots of chat on the forum, Motorhome Fun about this.

Below is a photo of our American 'C' Class, at a lay-by in France during our 2007 trip. You can see the car is attached by an 'A' Frame. Sometimes the car is described as a toad in this instance.

Nowadays, as I have already mentioned, we have standard bikes and sometimes tow Mike's scooter on a trailer. We also walk and use public transport. All these options save having to move the motorhome off a pitch in order to go exploring.

Left or Right-Hand Drive?

We spend most of our time in continental Europe and felt it would make sense to have a left-hand drive vehicle. As I mentioned earlier, our current base vehicle is a Citroen Jumper (the left-hand drive version of the Relay). The headlamps and speedometer needed to be modified to meet legal requirements in Britain. The original dial displayed kilometres, not miles, and the headlamps were aligned to drive on the right hand side of the road, not the left as we do in the UK.

Large vs. Small

Size is important and there are pluses and minuses. Here's my list:

Benefits of a Large Motorhome :)

• A true home from home set up.

• Large cupboards and lockers to pack what you need.

• Full sized domestic appliances, such as microwave oven, fridge freezer, and air conditioning.

• Separate bedroom.

• Greater headroom and the ability to spread out.

• More area inside with the addition of slide outs.

• Large powerful engine. Great work horse for towing and steep inclines.

• Luxury campsites, some with serviced pitches for water and sewage. Even cable TV.

• Huge capacity tanks for fresh water, grey water and effluent.

• Suitable for conversion to run on liquid propane gas (LPG), therefore saving on fuel cost.

• Built to carry a high laden weight (payload).

• Room to spread out inside for close friends and family to visit or stay.

Downsides of a Large Motorhome :(

• Too big for many European roads.

• Difficult to park and manoeuvre.

• Difficult to find large enough pitches.

• Navigation nightmares.

• High running costs and high fuel consumption.

• Some legal 'grey areas' concerning tow frames and size of motorhome itself.

• May have to take HGV test.

Benefits of a Small Motorhome :)

• Built and designed for European roads and campsites, gives freedom to explore.

• Manoeuvrable and relatively easy to park.

• Easier to find somewhere to stay.

• Home from home in miniature.

• Good fuel economy.

Downsides of a Small Motorhome :(

• Limited capacity for waste and freshwater tanks.

• Smaller cupboards.

• Reduced payload. (Which means you have to take less with you).

• Difficult to dry items, when access to outdoor drying isn't possible.

• Risk of claustrophobia.

Conducting Research

There are several magazines available and you can use these to get a flavour of motorhoming and compare different specifications. These include Motorcaravan Motorhome Monthly (MMM) available as a paper edition or digital. Which Motorhome, Practical Motorhome, Motorhome and Campervan. MMM have also published a guide to help you buy a used motorhome.

Go to the showrooms. Look inside the brand new models on display as well as the selection of used vehicles.

Attend motorhome shows, they're staged all over the UK each year and include the Motorhome and Caravan Show at the National Exhibition Centre in Birmingham, in February and October.

If you have the inclination and time, consider going to the Düsseldorf Show in Germany, held at the end of August. It's not strictly necessary for research, but it's the largest in Europe and potentially the world. You can see a vast selection of motorhomes and gadgets there.

Düsseldorf is a pleasant city in its own right and so you could combine visiting the show with a city-break or a short holiday. There is an enormous campsite set up for the show every year. It's in the grounds of the exhibition centre.

Some people purchase a vehicle in Europe and import it back into Britain.

Once you have drawn up a list of features and layouts that you like, consider borrowing a motorhome from a friend for a mini-break or hiring one. Justgo motorhomes hire out vehicles throughout the UK, Europe, New Zealand and Australia.

Consider staying close to your house for the first trip, in case you forget any essentials. Make a list as you go along of likes and dislikes.

Have a look at websites managed by experts and don't be afraid to make contact and ask for advice. One of my favourites is Magbaz Travels. This has been compiled by Barry and Margaret Williamson who have been cycling and motorhoming for more than twenty years. They have over seventy fellow travellers who contribute regularly to the website, the idea being that long-term, long-distance travellers by motorhome and/or bicycle should freely share their knowledge, experience and advice. There are hundreds of articles and thousands of photographs, which also includes a comprehensive A-Z Guide to motorhoming

The forums provide tips based on the experiences of others. The quality does vary. I think it's a bit like having a conversation with a bloke down the pub. There's loads of really useful stuff as well as gossip. Forums shouldn't be overlooked because no question goes unasked. Here are some; Motorhome 365, Motorhomefacts, Motorhomefun, Outandaboutlive, and Wildcamping.co.uk.

Where to buy

Private sale, classifieds or in the magazines, eBay, dealerships or at a show. Have a look at new and pre-loved vehicles to help decide your favourite features.

How to buy

If you're a talented mechanic you could buy an elderly vehicle at a bargain basement price, and be prepared for potential ongoing maintenance and breakdown issues.

Older vehicles will fall foul of recent legislation regarding engine emissions and vehicles with diesel engines manufactured before 2002 are not allowed in London and in several other European cities because of emission controls. The AA (Automobile Association) website has information on the Low Emission Zones (LEZ).

We have experienced teething problems with each one of our motorhomes. Bear this in mind and make sure you test all the systems and appliances extensively before departure. Some of our discoveries have been made when we have been hundreds of miles away from home. Don't book a ferry until you have thoroughly tested the base vehicle and performed extensive habitation checks. Delivery dates for your new baby often run beyond the original gestation period and the fact that you have a holiday booked will do nothing to speed up the process.

It is possible to borrow money in order to buy your motorhome. Finance companies are advertised at the motorhome dealerships, in the magazines, or you could have a look at Pegasus who specialise in providing motorhome finance.

Chapter Two
Everyday Essentials

In the western world we are fortunate that our basic needs for food, water, sleep and maintaining our body temperature can be met and most of us take them for granted. They also form the foundation for all other human requirements. Many people would like to see Wi-Fi included here, as a fundamental for survival, but I cover that later.

I'm going to talk about food first. It's a subject close to my heart and I'm infatuated by it, in fact, I struggle to find a calorie I dislike.

Food

A motorhome comes equipped with a fridge as standard. They vary in size depending on the age and size of the base vehicle. Some motorhomes have a full sized fridge-freezer, others, little more than a powered cool-box. They can run using gas, mains or 12 volt electricity. Some 12v fridges only supply power while the engine is running, whereas others function even when the engine is switched off. This is important because you could end up with a flat battery if you were parked for a long time with no additional source of power.

Remember to lock the fridge and use storage containers with a lid. (The plastic boxes from takeaway food are a perfect size.) We were driving the length of Mexico's Baja peninsula in our European 'C' Class, Mike drove round a sharp bend, and whoa - the fridge door swung open. I didn't know that the catch had broken, and our leftover rice from supper the night before now covered the carpet.

Mike and I are not vegetarians, but we are in the van. A few years back we decided to eat less meat for health reasons, and an ideal way of doing this was not to have it available in the motorhome. As we enjoy eating out, we could feed the inner carnivore at a restaurant. This has brought additional benefits for the practicalities of motorhome life. There is less risk of harmful food spoilage with vegetarian foods - i.e. fish or meat going off. Keeping the van clean is easier because meat fat spits, and so I have found that the oven doesn't get as grimy. Unlike vegetable oils, meat fat becomes thick and 'claggy' when cold. This makes the washing-up more difficult, even the washing-up bowl gets greasier. I know this because we do lapse and have the occasional meat meal.

As for what to cook, we eat as normal. All our favourites from toast to toad-in-the-hole (veggie sausages). We do a lot of one pot cooking, such as chilli, bolognese and stews, reheating the leftovers the following day.

I enjoy perusing the shelves of grocery shops while we're away to see what foods are available and usually can't resist buying some local speciality. At a later date I can look through the food cupboard in the van and get a kick out of seeing the different labels and languages on the various bottles, jars and tins. This reminds me of where we have been, and helps you realise how far my obsession with food extends.

You need to take all the items you use at home for food preparation and eating. We only have what we use - 2 saucepans with lids, 1 small frying pan, 1 lasagne dish, 1 roasting tin, 1 Yorkshire pudding tin, 1 grill pan, 2 chopping boards, 2 bowls, 2 plates, 2 glasses, 2 mugs, 1 large and 1 small cafetière, 1 knife, fork and spoon each, coasters and mats; plus the assorted requirements for food preparation including sharp knives and cheese grater. This means that if you come round for a coffee you need to bring your own mug.

When we first started out we bought plastic glasses and melamine plates but because we prefer china and real glass we got rid of them. Some motorhome owners use enamelware, which I have been told can be put in the oven to warm up and doesn't break or rattle. Mike can't stand jangling noises when we drive, so I pack the cupboard contents in bubble wrap and protect the base with rubberised mesh wrap. I sandwich squares of cardboard between the plates and bowls. This doesn't look pretty, but he doesn't grumble and if anything has got smashed it has been due to my clumsiness.

Water

A motorhome has a fresh water tank on board, usually between 70 and 100 litres in capacity. Ours has 100 litres and lasts three to four days. The tank is filled by attaching one end of a hose to a tap, the other fits into a water inlet on the motorhome. We dumped our hose after the first trip because we found it impossible to secure it to most taps as all the fittings were different. Mike now uses a ten litre plastic watering can with a spout that fits the water inlet. It takes a while to fill the tank in this way, but one of his favourite sayings is "Time's what I've got". You may not have the will, health or fitness levels required to lug watering cans and so you should look at taking different tap adaptors to go with a hose. Consider jubilee clips and bath/kitchen adaptors for domestic taps. I looked up hose/tap adaptors and as there are so many to choose from, I can see why Mike resorted to a watering can.

You need to be careful where you get your water from, it may be polluted with salt water or worse. Many owners don't drink the water from their on board tank at all. Mike reuses 6 litre water containers for carrying water, the 8 litre bottles are too heavy.

Our American RVs had a water filtration system provided as standard, but most motorhomes can have one fitted. This needs extra research because there are several types and the integral filter needs to be changed at regular intervals.

In our current motorhome we do drink the water from our tank but drain it completely if it's been standing for more than three or four days. Occasionally we flush the pipes and tank through with a weak bleach solution. Perhaps we may live to regret drinking from our tank as there is no way of knowing if the fresh water has become contaminated.

Below is a photo of Mike collecting water from a spring during our month long visit to Corfu in 2003. He was using buckets back then because we could fill our fresh water tank from inside the van. It had a lid at the top that we could unscrew and was housed underneath one of the dinette seats.

When we went to Russia and Belarus we only drank filtered water from our friends' motorhome as these countries are known to have polluted supplies. If we hadn't had access to this we would have bought bottled water.

Power Options

In a house, electricity is simple, you use it, and all being well, pay the bill at the end of the month. In a motorhome it is a little more complex because it's possible to live independently of a mains electric supply using power from a variety of sources.

I'm not qualified to give expert and technical guidance on electrics or gas issues. Fortunately there's lots available to read in books, magazines and on the internet because it can get complicated and confusing.

Here are a few tips to get you started.

Mains Electricity

You arrive on a campsite, find the electric hook-up point (EHU), attach one end of your own cable to their outlet, the other to the input on your motorhome and you have mains power supplied inside. All the appliances work as they would at home.

If you visit campsites in continental Europe you will need an adaptor because their hook-ups are different to ours in Britain. A three pin adaptor for the UK is also useful for if you are parked at a house.

You need to be careful not to have all your electrical appliances switched on at the same time as you could blow a fuse and trip the circuit, worse still the whole site. (Yes, it's happened to us.)

In some countries there is an issue with polarity. This can cause problems on board and we have a polarity checker which we plug into one of our sockets inside. As this is done, a series of lights illuminate to inform us of any polarity issues. It's to do with the flow of electric current and there are technical manuals that explain it in detail.

If we are paying for electric hook up, we use electric appliances to save our gas. We have a toaster, 800W kettle and small 900W oil-filled electric radiator.

Generator

If you don't have a mains supply, or the one supplied is inadequate (sometimes less than 6 amps is provided overseas) and you need more power, you can purchase a generator. Some motorhomes have one fitted, but when we had one we only ever switched it on once a month for maintenance. We found it too noisy and didn't want to be unsociable.

12 Volt

This is the electricity supplied from a vehicle battery. Many appliances are powered or recharged using a 12v supply. Most new cars have at least one socket for DVD players and other portable devices, and as the demand has risen more gadgets have become available that use 12v.

In order to prevent the engine battery in a motorhome becoming continually drained, additional leisure batteries are usually fitted. These receive charge from the engine and after a long drive last up to three days. They will also recharge when the motorhome is hooked up to mains electricity.

Another way to recharge the leisure batteries is to have a solar panel, ours is 130Watts. It is stuck to the roof with marine adhesive. This charges up our two leisure batteries - 115 Amp Hour (AHR) Banner Bull (95901). This set up enables us to park for extended periods of time without EHU. We once spent a month on a car park, solely using 12v and didn't flatten the engine battery.

Some appliances won't work or recharge using 12v and for these you need to consider an inverter. You can buy a portable, or have one fitted to your motorhome permanently. A specialist in vehicle electrics can advise on the most appropriate one to meet your needs.

RoadPro stock all types of electronic goods for on the road use.

Lighting

The lighting in modern motorhomes is provided by Light Emitting Diode (LED) bulbs. They use a small amount of electricity, and this helps the batteries keep their charge for longer.

We have also fitted additional lighting underneath the bed so that we can find things in the dark.

Gas

The cooker, fridge, central heating and hot water system in our motorhome use gas. The fridge and hot water system can also run using electricity when we're hooked up to the mains. Some motorhomes have an outlet for a gas barbecue.

There are a variety of storage options for gas. These include a refillable LPG tank fitted onto the motorhome at the time of manufacture; cylinders that you buy and exchange and refillable cylinders by Gaslow.

You need to have an annual habitation check performed to check gas safety. We use, on average, 0.75 litres of gas a day when we don't have electric hook up.

Our van conversion had a 20 litre tank when we bought it but we wanted a larger one, and had a 30 litre fitted to give us longer between fill-ups. This was because we found LPG difficult to obtain in Spain. This has changed in recent times. Fuel stations and depots that stock it are listed on the Spanish website, Ircongas. I have listed this in the web links section at the back.

When we went to Greece in 2011, fuel stations that sold it were few and far between, but that may have changed now.

Grey Water

This is used to describe water that has been used for showering or washing-up. Our current motorhome has a grey tank fitted with 100 litre capacity.

When this gets full it needs to be emptied in to a proper drain. Don't let is gush all over a field, or car park, nor over the road as you drive. This may seem tempting but this water is dirty and contains chemicals from various products including detergent and shampoo. You need to empty it from your motorhome into a receptacle, then tip it down a main drain. If passers-by see you throwing buckets or washing-up bowls into laybys or verges they may get upset because they don't know if you're up to no good.

You need to look after your grey tank because the stale water can get excruciatingly smelly, especially in hot weather. Empty it regularly, don't let food debris or grease go down the plug hole, as this could block the pipes. Try not to discard the cooking water from potatoes, rice or pasta because when cool, the starch forms a coating on the inside of the tank which becomes ultra-smelly.

If we're on a campsite, I strain the cooking water into a jug and throw it down (the water, not the jug) the waste water drain. If we don't have access to one of those we use a funnel to pour it into an empty two litre plastic drinks bottle. This we then pour down the next drain we come across.

Before we do the washing-up Mike wipes the dirty dishes and used cutlery with kitchen paper in order to 'pre-clean' it all before a proper wash in soapy water.

Drain freshening chemicals can be used to pour down the plug holes but we have found these unnecessary. We try and empty the grey tank daily, keeping the tap open when it's empty and not in use. We also pour a weak bleach solution down the plug holes from time to time to keep the pipes 'fresher'.

Black Waste

This is another way of saying sewage. The big RVs have a large tank fitted and these need to be emptied at approximately two week intervals. There are specialised containers, with wheels, to drain the waste into, which can then be tipped into a sewage drain or chemical toilet disposal point.

If your motorhome has a holding tank, you can buy a macerator to pump the sewage and this would be useful if you can't get close enough to a dump point.

When we owned an RV we bought our accessories at Mobile RV in Oxfordshire.

The smaller European motorhomes have what is called a cassette. This is a plastic container that slides and locks into position underneath the toilet. A cassette usually, but not always, has a 20 litre capacity. Unfortunately, ours fills up too quickly, so we use public toilets where we can, but for many motorhome owners emptying the cassette is a daily chore.

Biodegradable toilet paper is available to help prevent blockages. After emptying, a chemical fluid is measured into the cassette to eliminate unpleasant smells, reduce gas build up, stimulate the breakdown of waste matter and toilet paper, and keep the tank clean.

Access to the cassette is usually through a small door on the outside of the van. Never, ever, ever, empty the cassette anywhere other than a chemical toilet waste disposal point, a domestic toilet or into a sewer. It is horrible, but some inconsiderate people tip their black waste into the sea, rivers, waste ground or bury it. This is unacceptable behaviour, gives motorhomers a bad name and upsets people for all the right reasons.

A motorhoming newbie once commented that he found dealing with sewage particularly abhorrent – he described it as "having to deal with the 'poop' twice".

The access door for our toilet cassette is located inside the van, which is unconventional, but hasn't proved to be a problem.

Keeping Clean

Only the most basic motorhomes and day vans lack a shower with hot and cold water. The water is heated using the on board gas system or mains electricity, if you're hooked up.

To avoid continual fresh water tank fill ups, you should shower yourself with plain water, turn off the tap, then soap up, and switch the tap on again to rinse. Many campsites have shower facilities as well. If I use a public shower I always wear rubber soled shoes such as flip-flops or Crocs. This is because I'm squeamish about other pairs of feet that have stood on the shower tray. My suspicions were validated by an infection control nurse recently who told me that different infectious conditions of the feet can be spread by sharing public facilities.

We have a supply of wet wipes to use if we're running low on water.

Our shower and toilet are inside a wet room, with a sliding door to prevent water splashing in the living area. The shower tray is built onto a solid base to prevent flexing. After a shower we have to dry the floors, walls and toilet with a soft absorbent cloth. This has become part of the routine and means another daily activity takes a few minutes longer because we're in a motorhome.

Cleaning Inside the Motorhome

This is blissfully quick compared to normal housework. I use standard domestic products and cloths. I find the wet wipe type of cloths useful for surface cleaning, particularly the bathroom and windows. We have a removable carpet on the floor, which I sweep at least once a day with a stiff bristled, short handle brush. If we're staying with friends I take out the carpets, hoover and clean them.

Laundry

When we first started out in 2002 we used laundrettes. Mountains of laundry would pile up and we would take a day to get it all done. Launderettes have become expensive and so we have considered how to make this necessity cheaper.

For a practical approach to managing wash loads, consider colours. If you don't take whites you save on a separate wash and staying with neutral shades helps to prevent clothes dye running, and reduces the number of loads.

Another tip to reduce the size of the washing pile is to use a flat bed sheet underneath the duvet cover, this then needs washing less frequently.

Mike wears hiking gear and although I can't stand the sludgy colours, for him, they're practical, easy to wash and dry and we don't have any ironing.

For several years we had a plastic twin tub washing machine. It was designed for camping and brilliant. We eventually sold it because Mike took to hand washing instead. His choice, he's a domestic God.

He enjoys winding people up with hard luck stories that I don't do any chores at all and he is harangued by a bully of a wife. This poor long suffering man has made it all into a routine and he enjoys the reaction he gets from men of different nationalities.

On several occasions Mike has been approached while doing the laundry, by a fellow male who has been shaking their head, while simultaneously wagging their index finger from side to side and muttering 'no' in their language or quietly tutting. Mike's response is to smile innocently and ask,

"Isn't it like this in your country?"

I can only presume each one is chauvinistic about 'women's' work and trying to stop Mike before 'the wife' gets to see him in action.

If you do decide to go down the hand-washing route don't be tempted to hang washing out in car parks; it offends the locals and you're likely to get moved on. Remember to think how you would feel if you saw motorhomes parked near your home and they had all their washing out to dry. We once saw a domestic washing machine being used on a car park. The wire stretched across the road to a generator that was on the ground next to a neighbouring van.

The photograph below was taken by a German lady on the campsite in Albufeira, Portugal. She couldn't believe that anyone, let alone a man, could be so enthusiastic about getting the washing done.

For my last laundry based anecdote, Mike was once doing some hand washing, when he got chatting to an inquisitive Dutch lady. She was fascinated because she used the same techniques as him. I don't know what their methods were to induce such levels of excitement, perhaps swirling the water in the same direction, or an equivalent number of rinses, whatever it was these laundry soul mates had found each other and we ended up exchanging email addresses.

Sleep

If a motorhome doesn't have a permanent bed, the daytime living area is used for sleeping and so not only do you both have to go to bed at the same time, but also reconstruct and remake it each night. As full-timers we would find this detrimental for our ability to share such a small space.

With our first motorhome, and our current one, we can't walk around the bed. This means that if I need to get up when we're both in bed, I have to climb over Mike to get out. This isn't a problem for us, but it may be something to consider if you're less mobile or have to get up several times during the night.

Do you remember the fairy tale, 'The Princess and the Pea'? She couldn't sleep unless her bed was perfectly comfortable. Comparisons can be drawn with Mike and his attitude towards a comfy bed.

The original mattress supplied with the van was the same as the base of the dinette seat, covered in upholstery fabric that matched the seating in the rest of the van. After four years it was becoming uncomfortable as it was less firm and we were aware of the creases running widthways underneath the bottom sheet when we were in bed. We had covered the Wildax base with a large piece of memory foam, cut to the right size. We have now got a custom made memory foam mattress from the Memory Foam Warehouse. It is slightly thicker and so we're now raised a little bit higher. This means that Mike's hair brushes the overhead cabinets when he gets in and out of bed.

It sometimes gets extremely cold at night. If we have electric hook-up, we sometimes use an oil filled radiator. It's 900W and we keep it on a low setting.

We have a removable carpet which we keep over the laminate floor all year round. This helps combat the cold coming through the floor.

The walls are covered with a thick insulating material and it's usually between two and four degrees warmer inside than out.

When we're away we sleep really well and as I wake up it takes me a few seconds to realise where I am. This may be because we move location frequently, or it may be the fresh air, or effective blackout blinds, making it pitch dark inside when they're closed.

Mike has a bad back and if we're not level he doesn't sleep well. When we first arrive somewhere it takes him ages to decide if the van is parked to his satisfaction. We use a spirit level to make sure we're really flat and if we're at a designated motorhome parking spot we use levelling blocks underneath the wheels. These are made from heavy duty thick plastic and provide a wedge shaped ramp to drive the wheel up on to. The leading brands are Fiamma and Milenco.

Avoid parking close to busy roads and be aware that campsites can be noisy during the summer, particularly in Mediterranean countries where the holidaymakers seem to keep partying all night long.

Another of Mike's show time routines for fellow campers is to open up the rear doors and delve into his understores, while I'm still in bed. I like to stay tucked up under the covers and read when it's cold outside and Mike likes to get a reaction from others. I think they seem more shocked that I'm not bothered about what he's up to as I give them a quick wave, sunny smile and get on with the next chapter.

Air Conditioning

Our American motorhomes had air conditioning installed as standard; however we didn't use it and chose not to have it fitted to our current vehicle. I don't like it because for some reason it makes my knees ache as well as making my eyes and nostrils feel dry. When a unit is switched on it increases fuel consumption when driving and we prefer trying to acclimatise to the heat.

The summer can be pretty stifling and many motorhomes head north during these hot months to avoid the high temperatures.

Entertainment

We specified a 17" flat screen TV in our van conversion, rather than their standard 14". We also insisted that it should have a headphone socket so that if one of us wants to go to bed early, they can go to bed in peace and quiet, while the other continues to watch and listen.

If we're both watching TV we plug an external speaker into the headphone jack because the sound quality of the built in one is poor.

Using a memory stick, we can pause and record live television, look at photographs and video files. We can also connect our high definition TV to the laptop using an HDMI (High Definition Media Interface) cable.

I read using an e-reader because I find it convenient to download books and read them straight away. I've got hundreds of titles, a life-time supply - I don't think I'll ever get to read them all. As a techno-phobe Mike prefers paper books.

Payload

I'm unable to describe payload in depth, however my understanding is that it's the weight that is carried on your motorhome after the weight of the vehicle itself has been deducted - (i.e. the laden weight).

It is illegal to be overweight and all too easy to become so. Because our Wildax had extras fitted that would add to the overall weight and because we carry all our gear for year round use, Mike didn't want us to exceed the maximum legal weight.

Our vehicle has been re rated from 3500 kg (3.5 Tonne) to 3950kg by SvTech. This was possible because our base vehicle has reinforced rear twin leaf suspension and has the capability to take the extra weight.

It is a good idea to fit proper motorhome tyres if the van is to be left standing for long periods.

Tools

We carry a basic tool box in a case as well as a small axe to chop firewood and a military style folding spade which we have used to try and dig ourselves out of sand. (More on that incident later.)

Pets

For me, a house is not a home without a cat and this one of the few things I miss about not having a permanent base. When we so selfishly hit the road back in 2002 we had two moggies, Mickey and Dave. Friends of ours took them in and they successfully re-trained their humans.

As we have never taken a pet with us for any of our travels I can't give experiential tips on what to do. However, I do know that planning is required to take an animal overseas. It's a good idea to get the wheels in motion, undertaking the research well in advance of making any trips, because it's time consuming getting organised.

Information is on the Department for Environment, Food and Rural Affairs (thankfully that mouthful is abbreviated to Defra) website.

When a pet returns to the UK they need to be given a clean bill of health by a vet before setting off from the continent, so that they have been examined within 24 hours of arriving back in Britain.

I have heard that the vets nearest Calais are more expensive. It's worth asking other owners where they go within a 24hr radius of the port. We have friends who go to one near Boulogne the day before their crossing.

Some people take a dog for security, others take a pet to keep them company. This year we saw a couple of parrots, a cat and several dogs. Cats are usually trained to use a lead.

We saw one on a campsite at El Rocio in Spain. He was accustomed to roaming free and it was clear that he wasn't traumatised by this in any way. However, we did notice the owner struggling to persuade him back to the van at departure time.

As we're inquisitive, we asked the owner if this was always the case when it became time to leave. He admitted that his cat remembered that site because they had been a few times before. He really loved it there and a routine had developed where his moggie would scamper from van to van, evading capture and trying to remain elusive when he could judge that it was 'that time' again.

Bugs

Insects, midges, mosquitoes and what Mike calls 'biters' are a nuisance. Motorhomes have a fly screen fitted over each of the roof vents and windows. Unfortunately, we didn't have one on the large sliding door when we bought our van but we managed to get one for a left-hand drive vehicle sourced from Reimo in Germany and had it delivered to us in the UK. It is attached to the van with poppers and Velcro and has a zip up entrance. They became prohibitively expensive after we bought ours.

Other van conversion owners have modified and fitted one made by JML. I have been told that Wilko, Homebase and BHS stock them, but I haven't seen one in any of those shops.

Another idea is to hang a large net curtain over the doors. This can also be used to cover the back doors, which can then be opened on a hot night and allow circulation of air. My attempt at making one using a piece of nylon netting was shameful.

The photo below is of Pearl, she's parked at a beach in Greece and you can see the fly screen is fitted.

Tips for Storing the Motorhome

If the van is not going to be used for a while, we follow the manufacturer's instructions for storage. This includes draining all the tanks, (hot and cold water, and fresh) emptying the toilet cassette and cleaning the oven, stainless steel surfaces and food cupboards.

We eat up foods that could attract ants and other insects. Any containers with jam, chutney or similarly sweet that we can't finish ourselves we give away.

I defrost and clean the fridge, taking all the shelves out. I use warm soapy water with bicarbonate of soda dissolved in it. I use a soft cloth for the initial clean and wipe it dry with paper kitchen towel. Then I splash spirit vinegar in water and wipe that on all the internal surfaces.

While we are away I keep the freezer compartment wedged open, as well as the door. A tip from the British Army (Mike's son) is to put unused tea bags inside the fridge to absorb any moisture. These steps all prevent mould growing, tried and tested.

The finale for the fridge is something you don't want to witness me undertake. My frustration levels reach new heights, because our model has the most awkward shelves. They are held inside with clips on the edges of the shelves and these slide into grooves on the plastic sides of the fridge. For some reason, getting them back after cleaning is ridiculously difficult and must have been designed by someone who wasn't thinking that after removing them, they would need to be put back again. I don't swear, it doesn't sound nice, but this justifies foul language.

Pre-Departure Check List

In order to avoid potentially expensive mistakes, such as forgetting to retract the electric step or failing to wind in the awning, Mike has written a check list and laminated it. He lays it over the driver's foot pedals when we arrive somewhere new so that he can't fail to see it before we leave. I have reproduced it on the next page.

CHECK LIST

Internal

• Secure All Items.

• Lock Fridge.

• Lock Seats to Front.

• Secure Back Storage Area.

• Check Cupboards All Locked Down.

• Close All Roof Vents.

• Close All Windows.

• Fridge to Battery.

External

• Retract Step.

• Disconnect Power Cable.

• Check Rear Door Locked.

• Empty Grey Tank.

• Top-up Fresh Water Tank.

• Check Underneath Van.

• Washing Line.

What goes on the list is all down to preference, many don't have one, and when Jon (as in the naming of our van) saw Mike's list, he got to work and prepared one in his honour - it's on the opposite page.

CHECK LIST

Internal

• Secure All Items. (Ensure all labels are facing forward.)

• Lock Fridge. (Double check, clean front and sweep floor.)

• Lock Seats to Front. (Handbrake off), hoover and wash.

• Secure Back Storage Area. (Do stock take.)

• Check Cupboards All Locked Down.
  (Add items to shopping list in short supply.)

• Close All Roof Vents. (Check weather.)

• Close All Windows. (Wipe down with cloth.)

• Fridge to Battery. (Disinfect switch after doing so.)

• Check Alignment of Baked Beans.

External

• Retract Step. (Wash prior to retraction with dilute bleach.)

• Disconnect Power Cable. (Wrap in precise figure of 8 with 23cm overhang at each end.)

• Check Rear Door Locked (Proceed to A&E.)

• Empty Grey Tank. (Bleach and clean and disinfect and wash and clean and wash more then re-clean and if possible steam clean.)

• Top up Fresh Water Tank. (Measure into tank with litre jug.)

• Check Under Van. (Re-grease joints.)

• Washing Line. (Wipe down and carefully wrap in neat figure of 8 before forgetting where it should live.)

Chapter Three
Safety and Security

Vehicle Insurance

As with any vehicle, you must have adequate insurance cover for a motorhome. If you're travelling abroad you will need a permanent UK address. Most companies provide cover for six months a year but some do a full twelve. You should check which countries are covered on a green card and some policies include breakdown cover. Read the small print and check your entitlements when away from the British Isles. The German Automobile Association (ADAC) provides cover for British residents.

The AA publish a country by country guide to driving abroad, which you can access on their website. It's worth having a look before you leave as requirements change all the time.

We have renewed our vehicle insurance and tax online while we have been away.

MOT

Once your vehicle reaches the age of three it has to have an MOT (Ministry of Transport) test every twelve months and you need to bring it back to the UK in order to get it done. It's a nuisance, but has to be built into your motorhome year, or this could affect the insurance. We turn this into an opportunity to visit friends and family and time it for the summer to improve our chances of better weather.

If you are in Britain you can get an MOT done at any time to give another twelve months of motorhoming.

Health Insurance

Make sure you research cover carefully and check you have a valid European Health Insurance Card (EHIC) before you leave. This was previously called an E111.

We used Travel Nation for our trips outside Europe. They provide flexible all year round cover but have recently stopped providing it for pre-existing medical conditions. We made a couple of small claims through them, they paid up with no quibbles.

I have read that Endsleigh and Aria (through the Camping and Caravanning Club) are cheaper. You should also investigate what the Nationwide Building Society offer in conjunction with their accounts.

Specific Security Measures

The cab in a motorhome has a standard alarm system and there are savings to be made on insurance if you have a Thatcham Class 1 fitted.

Choosing a Suitable Location

There are lots of views and standpoints on motorhome safety and security. From our perspective we feel fortunate that in our twelve years of full-timing we have only been the victims of one robbery and two failed attempts. We know of these because we were inside at the time.

I don't want to sound gloomy, but opportunistic thieves lurk in all areas, and security is always an issue with any type of travel. You should exercise as much caution in a motorhome as you would visiting anywhere at home or abroad. The next few paragraphs are going to sound negative but you do need to remain vigilant. Never leave valuable items on display when you go out and consider purchasing a safe to hide in the motorhome (we have one built in).

A campervan contains a feast of electrical and technological gadgetry for a criminal to get their hands on. No matter how careful you are with locking up and setting the alarm, there is the potential for a determined thief to get in because most windows are plastic and the ones in the driving area are glass and can be smashed.

Before parking, have a good look at the surrounding area for signs of 'tattiness' and an unkempt environment. By this I mean that you should check for graffiti, broken glass on the ground, abandoned vehicles or ne'er do wells hanging about. Do the surrounding buildings look in a decent state of repair? If you get a gut instinct that it doesn't feel right then you shouldn't risk it. Try to park close to other motorhomes and if possible ask the occupants of neighbouring vans how long they are stopping for. If we're parked overnight anywhere other than a campsite we ensure the motorhome is facing the direction of departure, and ready to go, in case a quick drive away is required. We keep the mobile phone and clothes by the bed. I also make sure my handbag and any other valuables, such as a camera are hidden. We always do the washing-up and putting away before we go to bed.

Try and start looking for somewhere to stop over while you have plenty of daylight. Everything looks different after dark. Consider planning where you would like to stay so that tiredness doesn't interfere with your decision making. Campsites provide a secure environment and there is usually one of those nearby if you run out of steam and decide to stop on the spur of the moment.

We have only slept over at motorway services twice in 12 years because we read in a magazine that break-ins are common. Bear in mind that a perpetrator can make a quick getaway on the fast roads.

Some people keep a dog for security, because it will bark if it hears an unusual noise. If we are parked on a street we tie a heavy metal chain between the two front door handles on the inside of the van and padlock the two ends of the chain together. This forms a loop between the doors on the inside, making it impossible to open the doors from the outside.

A benefit of choosing a van conversion is that because the base is on a commercial vehicle all the doors have deadbolt locks, making the use of a chain not strictly necessary. However we believe it provides a visible deterrent but a determined thief could still smash their way in if they wanted to.

One afternoon, in 2003 we parked on a prom front in Spain. There was another camper alongside, and it looked safe for the night. It wasn't until we woke up the following morning we realised that someone had broken in and helped themselves to some valuables from my handbag. It seems incredible that this would have been possible while we were asleep inside, but it definitely happened.

There is a theory that criminals 'gas' the occupants of a motorhome prior to breaking in at night. The idea is that the inhabitants will sleep more soundly as they breathe the vapours of anaesthetic gas, therefore assisting thieves. Drugs of this type are usually administered in the controlled conditions of an operating theatre, using a vaporiser unit and mixed with nitrous oxide or oxygen which the patient inhales via a face mask.

Gases such as chloroform and ether were used for operations years ago, but these produce unpredictable results. The patient may suddenly wake up during proceedings and could also suffer from nausea and vomiting after administration. Other problems with these - if they are implicated - are that ether is highly flammable, (seen any exploding motorhomes lately?) and chloroform affects the heart. (Are there more heart attacks amongst caravan, motorhome and truck owners while they're asleep?)

I'm not sure which type of chemical is supposed to be used but the problem with the idea is that it's not like squirting a whiff of fly-spray at an insect; human beings are much bigger and this makes it all quite complicated.

I chatted to an anaesthetist about the possibility, and read the views of another on a forum. It seems unlikely because the gas would need to be evenly dispersed through the living space of the van, which would also have to be airtight in order to maintain the concentrations required to keep the victims asleep. Not only is that a lot of gas but a motorhome isn't airtight. How would the gas be introduced into the motorhome? Through a window? But then the environment wouldn't be airtight. Perhaps through an air vent? But how could you get enough into the motorhome that way?

Vehicle crime is quick and opportunistic, and all this sounds laborious and difficult. Then there are gas canisters and a vaporiser unit to consider and don't forget, the van is most likely to be in a car park. All this activity would look suspicious to passers-by.

It all sounds like a logistical nightmare for the criminal, but it's a compelling idea, perpetuated by the urban myth factor. We have friends who have told friends of theirs that after the incident in Spain, we were definitely gassed - we don't believe it ourselves.

If being gassed sounds like a terrifying possibility, stay on a campsite. There are gas detection alarms to fix inside a motorhome but we haven't bought one.

After our break in we reviewed our security and as a result of this purchased heavy duty chains to tie between the doors as explained above. Up until this point we hadn't set the alarm while we were inside as we hadn't felt it necessary to do so. After the event, we set the alarm and as it had a motion sensor we would deactivate it if we had to get up during the night.

I haven't provided citations for books so far, because what I have written is based on our life as it has panned out. However, although I haven't read it myself, I understand that The Motorhome Security Handbook by James Brown, provides valuable information on all issues relating to security.

The Motorhome

Chapter Four
Where to Stay

One of the best things about a motorhome is that you don't have to plan in advance where to stay if you don't want to; no need to check in and out of a hotel or guest house; no need to worry if the weather changes because you have a whole wardrobe of clothing choices with you.

There is no greater pleasure than stopping when you've had enough, or simply deciding to stay on the spur of the moment. However, if you have children with you, or haven't got much time, then you may have a different view on planning.

There are thousands of campsites to choose from at home and abroad. Joining a camping organisation brings member benefits and saves on fees. In the UK this includes The Caravan Club and The Camping and Caravanning Club. The ACSI scheme offers discounts out of season. Useful websites are UKCampsite.co.uk and overseas – Vayacamping. I use all of these when researching a campsite.

In Europe, provision is given for motorhome parking, often with a service point to take on fresh water and dump waste. They are called Aires in French, Sostas in Italian and Stellplatz in German. There are more springing up in Spain and Portugal, where many motorhomes head during winter.

Information for Aires, Stellplatzes and Sostas can be found in books and on the internet, complete with GPS co-ordinates. This isn't necessarily in English, but because symbols are used alongside a few words in that language, you should be able to work out what they mean. For example, the availability of water is usually represented with a simple picture of a tap.

For France, there is an excellent book with more than 6,300 locations. It is available from Maison de la Presse (a rough equivalent of our newsagents), for approximately €10.50 and includes a map.

Many Aires are free all year round but some charge in high season.

As well as using books and the internet you can usually find good places to stop by chatting to others. I can only remember information by writing it down and our map is covered in hieroglyphic markings as I write recommendations of places to stay and where we have been.

I have listed some websites at the back of this book that give GPS co-ordinates for Aires and free camping. They are an online resource and not available in print.

Mike prefers a 'proper' book and uses a marker pen to highlight text and book marks to keep his place.

There are a few campsites that accommodate RVs, some are purpose built with serviced pitches providing fresh water and a sewer. When we owned an RV we used the recommendations of others to find big enough campsites.

I take childish delight in not knowing what to expect next in life. Because Aires are not categorised or part of a star system in the same way as guest houses, hotels and lodges, the standard of each varies. My next short anecdote shows that we keep an adaptable approach with the varying standards I've mentioned.

We spent several weeks at Parque de Palmeira which is at Albufeira football club in Portugal. This provides marked parking spaces for approximately 100 motorhomes. This facility was in its infancy and while we stayed it was gradually being improved with new amenities. The ladies shower block had been given back to them as they'd had to share it with the men while their block was being built.

Early one morning Mike noticed that the gents block was finally open and so he went across for a shower. As he arrived at the entrance an entourage of men in suits was being shown how work was progressing by the office manager. He beamed as he saw Mike and urged him to go inside and prove to the 'suits' that the work was going according to their schedule. First past the post is written in Mike's DNA and so he didn't need to be asked twice.

The water was piping hot and in plentiful supply. However there was no shower rose and so the pipe poured a stream of water. It was also too low, so

Mike had to stoop to get his head wet as the water was landing on his chest. Cement dust dissolved into the water and the resulting goo oozed down the walls. There was no privacy because they hadn't got round to fitting a door to the outside world, nor was there a shower curtain.

There are two ways to view this story. One is with disgust and that no-one in their right minds should have even gone in there. What was the office manager thinking? How could he use Mike to prove that the facilities were finished when they weren't? We thought it was hilarious. We were paying the princely sum of €4 a night, this included Wi-Fi, mains electricity, fresh water, chemical toilet dump and a drain for grey water. At that price we wouldn't have expected a shower with an unlimited supply of hot water anyway. However, some of our fellow campers became extremely irate because if the facility was offered, they felt that it should be in full working order. They didn't waste any time getting their complaints across in the office. We were able to take a more 'C'est la vie' approach as we have experienced far rougher treatment through the course of our travels.

We joined France Passion during our first year and this enabled us to stay free at vineyards and farms in France. One of our most memorable places was near Bergerac. We parked in front of the owners' farmhouse and I felt a bit shy because our van was obscuring their view. We were reassured that we were in the right place and went straight to the shop to buy some wine to drink that evening. Our view was of their vineyard, which stretched away from us to the horizon across rolling hills. As the sun set we sipped our wine, the flavour enhanced as we savoured a 'motorhome moment'.

France Passion has become so popular that the scheme has been extended to other countries and I have learned recently of a British version called Britstops. Mike and I were members of France Passion for a year. Friends of ours shared some of their feelings having been members – the other side of the coin, because they found some drawbacks. They noted that many farms were rural and isolated, with space for two or three campers. It took considerable navigating skills to find these farms because they were usually off the beaten track and to find they were full was disheartening.

Wild-camping is an expression commonly used to describe staying in a motorhome, off a campsite, perhaps on a car park or at the beach. Some people become upset about this being called wild-camping, as they regard it to be an inaccurate description because there's nothing wild about it. Other names for it are free camping or tolerated camping. Some people won't consider it because it seems to be dangerous and foolhardy to stay somewhere without the security of a campsite. Whatever your view, or what you choose to call it, if you do give it a go you should try and remain discreet and not look as though you are camping. Many people who take up motorhoming on a long term basis do wild-camp.

Mike and I decided to give wild-camping a try as soon as the opportunity presented itself. We were in Spain at the time and we saw a small group of motorhomes clustered together on a piece of rough ground. They were parked in a haphazard manner and we joined the group, leaving a space that we felt wouldn't be obtrusive.

Before we went to sleep that night I did feel a bit vulnerable because we were on an unguarded, unenclosed piece of land. I did wonder, as I dropped off, if I was acting in a foolish way but, when I woke up unscathed the following morning and having slept well, I soon forgot that I had ever been nervous about doing it.

It wasn't long before we met and chatted with others who did this on a regular basis and they told us about other suitable spots.

Stealth-camping probably describes what we do more accurately. We try and blend in with our surroundings, remaining as unobtrusive as possible. This is why Mike persuaded Wildax not to mark our van with any sign-writing. It makes it look more like a commercial van and less like a motorhome. When we're parked stealthily overnight we don't use the silver screen blackout blinds on the windscreen but hang a curtain up across the front. This is between the dashboard and the front seats.

In Spain and Portugal free camping is sometimes tolerated for longer than an overnight stop. These are mainly on large tracts of rough scrub land near the coast in Spain. The winter down south is a lot kinder than ours and if you do decide to head for one of these areas you will meet many like-minded folk from all over northern Europe. The local economy in some of these out of season resorts would collapse without motorhomes as the occupants buy their supplies from shops and markets. It also means that if you are on a restricted budget, you're avoiding campsite fees and saving a considerable amount of money throughout the course of a season.

However, nothing stays the same, perhaps a new mayor is appointed who doesn't have the same penchant for motorhomes as their predecessor. The last winter we had in Spain and Portugal there were so many motorhomes, in some areas it seemed like an infestation for the host country to deal with, because the facilities for dumping waste, obtaining fresh water and so on, aren't always available.

Remember to respect those in authority, and when visiting another country, you are a guest and subject to their rules and regulations, whether you agree with them or not. Also, spare a thought for the locals. How would you feel if you couldn't get parked in your home town, on market day because your regular car park was full of motorhomes? Not for a day or week, but a complete season. Try and support the local community by using the shops, restaurants, cafés and bars.

In Spain and Portugal you will find local people call in where motorhomes are parked in order to sell goods and provide services, such as laundry, bakery, fruit and honey. When we're far enough south I gorge myself on oranges in the winter, they taste so delicious compared with the long suffering fruits we get in British supermarkets. These must have travelled more miles than me, and not been allowed to ripen on the tree.

If we would like to stay overnight using a pub or restaurant car park, we ask the landlord (or whoever is in charge) before we order food, their permission to spend the night and have never been refused anywhere in the world.

Most of all, with a motorhome - if you can - take time, remember to relax and enjoy the drive. There's no need to rush and this type of travel is as much about the journey, as where to stop and stay. Potter along and only do a few miles a day, at this pace you're more likely to see the ideal spot to settle for a few hours, or possibly the night.

Trip Planning and Sightseeing

Many members of the motorhoming community choose where to go based on their hobbies. Fishing, hiking and different types of cycling are examples.

Mike has a keen interest in war history and although I don't share this in the same microscopic detail, we have explored battlefields over Europe and beyond.

We once met a couple who were passionate about bird watching on the Iberian Peninsula and they seemed to have visited nearly all of Spain's nooks and crannies to pursue their passion. Another gentleman, on his way to Morocco, followed the migratory route of birds heading south and this had taken him to Sub-Saharan Africa in his panel van on more than one occasion. Other travellers choose a theme for their tour; perhaps of historical interest or tracing the route of a river from its source.

Mike and I take an ad-hoc approach to sightseeing. Sometimes we do, sometimes we don't. It depends where we are and if we're in the mood. We're not avid art, history or religious types but we enjoy a wander around a new environment. In the early days I felt bereft without a guide book. After the first couple of years I realised that we had stumbled over our most memorable finds without a preceding fanfare from a book. Mike has always listened to the recommendations of others and read readers' travel articles in the motorhome magazines.

There is so much to appreciate in the world that I haven't got a bucket list. I get the most out of my explorations when I know hardly anything before the visit. When I read about it afterwards, it all seems to come together, because I can relate to what I have seen.

We tend to meander where the mood suits us and try to avoid making appointments in the diary. The most you'll get out of us regarding a future plan will be vague, perhaps we'll name a country or region. Avoiding being specific helps us to feel free without letting people down. Our decisions are often weather based as I hate being cold and Mike can't abide rain. He once put off joining friends to play golf two days in a row because the sky looked grey and there was a remote chance of a downpour. This earned him a new nickname of Fair-weather, which suits him. When deciding where to go on a trip it is worth considering the seasons. We stay as far south as we can during the winter and head north during the summer.

The coldest temperature we have ever experienced was in Derbyshire during an Arctic cold snap in December 2010. We were meeting friends to attend a carol concert and booked onto a local campsite. The wardens were concerned for our safety on their driveway as it had become extremely icy and slippery and so we asked the concert organisers if we could sleep on their car park. The snow was a foot deep and according to local reports the temperature had been dropping to -14°C overnight. We had extra blankets and kept the gas-fired heating on for the first night. When we woke up in the morning the heating had made our eyes and nostrils feel dry, similar to the effect air-conditioning has on me. The second night we decided to sleep without this on. I went to bed wearing thermal leggings and a long sleeved vest under my pyjamas. In the morning the temperature inside the van was a chilly -12°C, but warmer than outside.

When Mike removed the internal windscreen cover in the morning there was ice on the inside where condensation had frozen and he took a picture of it.

After the thaw we discovered that our water pipes had cracked and we had to have new ones.

During our trip to Turkey in 2012, we decided to surprise our German friends and join them at a beach. This way of life can be like a game and unfortunately the sand was deeper than we realised; ('Stuck in Sand – Miss Two Turns'). We were in the beach rather than on it, and couldn't dig ourselves out.

We broke the plastic tracks Mike put underneath the wheels and soon our knowledge of how to get out of such a situation was used up.

Luckily for us, a man on his tractor noticed, came over to have a look and was happy to haul us out. There are two photos taken on the day. The first is below and shows how deep in the sand we were, on the next page, is the second, taken a few minutes after we were towed out.

Chapter Five
Full-Timing

People that live in a motorhome, and use it as their home year round, are known as full-timers. We initially chose to do this for a year as we wanted to combine travel with Mike's semi-retirement and a motorhome seemed to provide ideal living accommodation to be able to do this. We didn't plan or imagine that it would be an ongoing lifestyle, twelve years later. We enjoy the freedom that travelling in a motorhome gives us, it enhances our life in a way that living in a house would not. I thrive on not knowing where I'm going to spend the next night and am unphased by packing, unpacking and repacking because it means a return to a favoured destination or exploring somewhere new.

It's not known how many people are full-timers, but we can't be confused with New Age Travellers or Gypsies; we aren't a part of an ethnic or religious group and are fully paid up and taxed members of society.

I do enjoy a break from the van from time to time but Mike never seems to need one, unless we've endured a lot of rainy days and he's been confined. After 12 years living full-time, I needed a longer break. I wanted to be a neighbour to my friends for a while and to feel like a part of their community. I also wanted to have a rest from the limited resources in a motorhome I first mentioned in Chapter 2. I needed long showers, unlimited broadband and the ability to have mains electricity all day, every day. This travel weariness can sneak up unawares and the six months off refreshed me and fired my enthusiasm for the next extended trip. The revelation of requiring a flat when living a 'charmed', life will sound as indulgent as our need for holidays; however, we aren't all made out of the same mould, and I am fortunate that Mike understood my needs and we could afford it.

Our way of life is often described as 'Living the Dream'. For many people this type of opportunity doesn't present itself until the traditional age for retirement, as this is the time when it becomes more financially viable - perhaps the mortgage is finally paid off, the kids have left home and the daily grind can cease, hopefully forever.

Without insulting the older generation, as George Bernard Shaw said,

"Youth is wasted on the young", perhaps retirement is wasted on the elderly, simply because the time and financial resources come when people aren't fit and well enough to go and fulfil their lifelong ambitions.

In order to cope with getting older and the fact that time isn't on our side, human nature is to get on with living and set goals for daily life. In the process we convince ourselves that this is our desired destiny and deny our dreams. If only we knew how long we had on the planet, planning would be so much easier.

As I mentioned in the first chapter, shortly after I met Mike we both realised that we shared a common life goal to travel. He was in the process of slowing down business-wise. He stopped looking for new contracts and along with good back-up at home we learned how to run his business from the motorhome. I have returned to work for a couple of stints over the past twelve years and we continued to live in the motorhome during this time. I finally hung up my work hat in 2010.

As I write this I can almost hear the chorus of "Oh, it's alright for you" from people for a variety of reasons and I count myself as lucky. However, seeing opportunities and acting on them would sum it up more succinctly. I don't have children, but if this were the case that wouldn't necessarily stand in the way and we have met others who combine motorhoming and family life with skill.

Mike planned to take early retirement when he was embroiled in what he describes as the "crazy days", when he worked round the clock as director of his own company. He set his goal for early retirement when he realised at a relatively young age that debt would be evil if it held him back from doing what he wanted. He thought it would steal his freedom.

There are many reasons not to seek a life change including money, circumstance, career, mortgage, pets and children, to name a few. Mike and I had all of those between us when we set off and now we can add grandchildren to the mix. However, I believe that procrastination is enemy number one in terms of life goal prevention, and that's hard to admit, because you only have yourself to blame.

If you're seriously thinking about living in a motorhome, you should write a pros and cons list for going ahead. Ask yourself some questions and bear in mind that your answers could be for real or possibly the dreaded procrastination.

You might have some of the following at home and miss them while away for extended periods; a garden, long hot showers, washing machine, dishwasher, a bath, pets, having a base, hoarding, sofa, open fire, central heating, large stereo system; Some of the white goods and home furnishings are available in a motorhome, but these would be the bigger ones with less flexibility for touring. Do you view these items as essential or nice to have? How far can you compromise for the ability to travel in a motorhome? You may want to return home for grandchildren, family get togethers or special life events.

You have to consider how you would feel if you don't try and bring your dreams to fruition. A pricey Axminster carpet, new kitchen or loft extension have never featured on my list of priorities. When I'm in my dotage, the carpet I gaze at is likely to be covered in questionable stains, but at least I'll be able to look at my photos or savour the memories of a life spent doing what I wanted.

When I looked up "Youth is wasted on the young" I stumbled across another George Bernard Shaw quote, which demonstrates his insight and eloquence, and sums up the essence of what I am trying to say:

"You see things; and you say, 'Why?' But I dream things that never were; and I say, 'Why not?'"

In order to fulfil the ambition to live full time in a motorhome, some people downsize their home, release equity, and buy something smaller, like a flat and rent it out. Others sell up completely, but if you take the plunge into that deep and scary pool, you need to consider what you would do if an unfortunate turn of events necessitated a return to 'normal' life in the UK.

Do you have supportive friends and family to stay with? Even without a disaster scenario you need to have back up at home, even if it's only someone to accept mail and parcels on your behalf.

If you think you may need a house for part of the year you could consider house sitting. If you do this make sure you have clearly agreed in writing what the expectations are for both parties. Do you need to work to boost finances or meet a higher purpose? Casual labour can be provided in return for food with schemes such as HelpX or Workaway. Travelling in a motorhome needn't be expensive and schemes such as these help a low budget go a long way. I met somebody recently who declared he wished he had £100,000 so that he could go travelling. His belief that he would require such a huge sum of money was blocking progress to achieve his goal.

Can You Make Room for Your Life Partner?

To full-time you need to be able to live in close quarters with your life partner. This may sound obvious but many couples would find this too stifling. It's not easy, but we make it work because we are living our common goal for a life journey, not pulling in opposite directions.

Mike and I enjoy a close friendship and like being in each other's company. I know it sounds corny but I love waking up next to him in the morning. I am fairly insufferable to most people first thing, as my eyes open and 'Bing!' I'm wide awake and ready for the off. In a similar vein Mike is like Tigger and matches my start speed.

We're not moody types, and prefer to keep a straight forward approach. If tensions are rising we know each other well enough to back down rather than have a confrontation, because there is no space. Avoiding mind games, we try to be honest with each other and this includes where we want to go, or what to do next.

Some of what you are reading may sound a bit too good to be true, and yes, if I'm honest there are definitely times when I do get really annoyed with Mike. I tell him he's getting on my nerves, and sometimes he stops doing whatever it was that was so irritating. I have developed the ability to ignore most of his wind-ups and irreverent sense of humour.

Tolerance and compromise are key ingredients. We have less floor space than a family bathroom or some types of prison cell and because of this only one of us can be moving about at the same time. This means that all our activities take longer than it would in a house or a larger motorhome. We can't even get dressed at the same time.

The little things in life become much more important. At one stage it seemed as though Mike always uttered "Where's my.....?" at the beginning of his sentences. One day, out of the blue, he invested in a 'man bag'.

This is a small, unfeminine canvas bag on a long strap. It is big enough for a notepad, pen, a neatly folded plastic shopping bag, wallet, keys and mobile phone. This minor addition removed a major irritation and resulted in a transformation in my attitude to his "where's my...?" questions.

Tidiness also has a role and I have had to learn this skill. In my single days I used to throw all my clothes out of the drawers and wardrobe onto the floor to find what I wanted to wear. The inevitable conclusion was that all my clothes would spend at least a month languishing where they had originally landed. I'm tidy now, completely cured because, it would be impossible to live like this in a van, everything has to be put away in the same place every time.

I'm not advocating that you must develop defined roles to live in a motorhome, but over the years we have gravitated towards those that match our core skills, or what we enjoy doing. As far as these go, I'm better at organising in the kitchen arena; food preparation, cooking, washing-up and putting away are all my department. I have learned more on the technical side for the computer, satnav and mobile phone; I jokingly refer to myself as the IT manager and Mike's personal secretary. Mike organises the budget, does the driving, clothes washing and shopping. He also finds fresh water, dumps the grey water and disposes of the toilet waste.

We don't live in each other's pockets, and I know this may sound unrealistic, but we do spend a fair proportion of each day independent of each other. We're not joined at the hip and often go for walks and bike rides on our own.

It's hard to say how we have managed to live so close together for such a long time, but I guess with analysis, it probably isn't as intense as 'outsiders' think. While we are away together, we co-habit in what we describe as a bubble, because our lifestyle keeps many of life's realities out of the way and we don't have distractions, such as the telephone, neighbours and so on. We can be selfish, meet our own needs and work out what we want to do for ourselves.

Life is a lot easier without an alarm clock and deadlines. Of course, life gets in the way sometimes and this has been clear when we have experienced vehicle breakdowns or family issues, but without the pressures of work, we have the time to be able to help out family and friends as well as wait for something to be mended on the van.

Time is a limited resource for us all, and we try to use it wisely, enjoying each day to the full. Mike and I avoid petty arguments and moodiness. We also try not to get caught up in minor issues. Neither of us deals well with confrontation as it's hurtful and difficult to unsay what's been hurled at each other during the heat of the moment.

I don't miss a house – neither does Mike. But when the thrill of exploring fades or the desire to go back somewhere dies, then of course we will start to wonder if we should continue this way. With the time, resource, health and the will to continue, this is us. If we stop having fun, we can analyse our situation and do something different.

If we think we have made a mistake and hindsight has told us a course of action wasn't such a good idea, one of my sayings is, "Well, if it were easy, everyone would do it."

Nothing in life is easy, but we can exercise choice and free will in pursuit of a full life and we both know how fortunate we are to be able to live the life we choose.

Chapter Six
Budget

The question of how much motorhoming costs and how to budget comes up regularly. It's difficult to give a specific figure as several factors are involved

If you would like to try and gauge how much money you need in order to plan for your new lifestyle, it's a good idea to keep a record of what you spend at home. Remember to write each item down, because it soon adds up.

Travelling in a motorhome becomes affordable if you can reduce your outgoings at home. As I mentioned in the last chapter, some people rent out their house, or sell it in order to release the equity. If you decide to do this don't forget to set aside some funds to cover storage costs for your belongings.

If you opt to rent out your property don't forget this is income, and each country has a tax requirement.

How much it costs depends on several factors; the kind of luxury and comfort you like to have; the number of miles you drive; whether you stay on campsites, Aires or free camp; if you cook in or go out for meals. If you have a low budget, travel slowly. Select a short itinerary or small region you'd like to visit rather that driving all over the map, or across a continent. This saves fuel and gives you more time to shop at markets and cook your own meals. You'll also be able to learn more about the locals this way and enrich the travelling experience.

Mike keeps a ledger and has, at times, been teased about this, because it's seen to be old-fashioned. He has kept a record of our spending since our first day on the road back in December 2002. He looks at the cost of fuel as well as exchange rates and uses the information for trip planning. He also records our average miles per gallon. When he is trip planning he can decide how much we need to cover our expenses, based on what we have spent in the past.

Mike's column headings in the ledger are; campsite, fuel, food, sightseeing, entertainment, ferry/flights, tolls/car-park, sundries and LPG.

Many people don't include ferries in their budget because it's not a daily spend. However, Mike does, because it helps him plan for the future and make a decision on whether to go somewhere for a short stay or a full season. He also adds up the annual costs of road tax, MOT, habitation check, servicing and insurance, as well as the fuel to drive back to the UK to get these chores done. He divides this by 12 and adds it to the monthly budget.

Our costs when we're in the UK are much higher than when overseas. This is partly because we catch up with friends and relatives, celebrating with meals and drinks out. It is also a time to make appointments; optician, dentist and prescription fees all add up.

We usually have a splurge with buying extra bits and pieces, either for ourselves or the van. I can't understand European clothes sizes and wouldn't want to waste time with shopping while we are away and so when we're back I take the opportunity to re-evaluate my wardrobe.

We also get online purchasing done, as we can use a UK address for deliveries.

Cost Comparison

As I mentioned in the chapter on full-timing we rented a flat for a short while when I needed a break from the van. This was during the summer of 2014 and gave us an ideal opportunity to compare the cost of living in a flat with a motorhome.

I had only been in the flat for 3 weeks when Mike was forced to curtail his trip to Germany and return to the UK. The driver of the car behind him hadn't been paying attention to the road ahead and rammed into our van from behind. This meant that Mike spent more than he had planned because there were additional fuel and ferry costs to get back to the UK as well as bed and breakfast accommodation while the van was being repaired.

The bottom line figure, for our comparison, not including ferries, eating out, sightseeing or the annual vehicle costs mentioned above, was £17 per day in the motorhome. This compares to £31 a day in the flat, which included rent, bills, public transport and socialising.

During June I noticed that there had been a spike in the 'Sundries' column. I looked back over the month and soon noticed that this had been due to the arrival of the birthday season. I bought presents for my youngest sister and niece. Both my parents had a birthday and I had an expensive haircut because it was my birthday as well. I hadn't realised I was spending extra at the time, but if your close family won't appreciate trinkets from a market stall, it's another factor to consider.

We have met individuals that do all their shopping in the UK for stores and supplies before they leave. They only shop on arrival for fresh food such as milk and vegetables. We enjoy eating out and this makes our spending budget unrealistically high for some.

If this is a way of life for you, remember it's not a holiday and so you need to be aware of ways to cut the costs of living and travelling overseas. I have found the Martin Lewis website has lots of useful advice on how to save, including which bank cards give better exchange rates.

When it comes to buying a motorhome it would be devastating to buy your heart's desire only to realise that you weren't completely satisfied with layout or cupboard space, for example, and this is why it's important to research thoroughly what your needs are when you make your choice.

Our experience with motorhomes has always been that they provide a home on wheels and Mike has looked at each vehicle as a long term option, similar to buying a house. The initial set up cost is high, but the longer you keep a vehicle the more this dissipates over time. We really noticed this when we decided that because of the repeated breakdowns we had no option other than to sell the coach in America. The long term plan became a short term one and this hit us hard financially.

Motorhomes are expensive, as I've said before, and we have lived in a couple of luxury vehicles with high running costs. Mike isn't a tycoon, he's worked hard and saved hard for what he has.

We once received a comment that our RV was ostentatious, which I found difficult to cope with at the time. I am aware that British people tend to champion the underdog, and some see an RV as a showy display of wealth. I have noticed that the majority of them are owned by people who have had their own business. Perhaps the personal qualities of an entrepreneur extend to going ahead and getting whatever you want in life. If this is the case, the owner will have worked extremely hard in order to get there, and this deserves celebration rather than denigration.

Success shouldn't be a breeding ground for resentment. I have sensed an undercurrent of jealousy amongst other Brits, almost as if it is more noble to live and travel on a shoestring.

Chapter Seven
Friendship and Family

Communication

Communication has evolved to such an extent that our experiences in the early days seem like a lifetime away. Way back then Mike wanted to run his office from the van and we had read that you could use a mobile phone as a modem.

As I've mentioned previously, Mike is a confirmed techno-phobe, not induced by fear but from hatred. He'd rather watch grass grow, or possibly stick pins in his eyes, than waste time in front of a computer.

As I am a supportive life partner, I was determined to see the mobile office project through. After days of perseverance, I'd used up all my tears of frustration and was finally forced to give up because our computer kept getting infected with a virus. (All I had needed to do was save his documents to a memory stick and use an internet cafe, but that revelation came with hindsight.)

About three weeks had elapsed when I noticed an elderly desk top computer, moulding away in the corner of the campsite office. The owner agreed to let me use it and I opened an email from a friend who was concerned about our whereabouts. We had forgotten to let anyone at home know how we were getting on. It wasn't that we didn't care, we'd been busy learning the ropes of our new life. When I replied to my friend I copied in everyone else in our address book and this led me to write a monthly newsletter in which I shared our exploits, a type of early blogging attempt.

The regular updates morphed into our first website, which I created in 2008. It enabled the folks back home to dip in and look at the photos and read about our experiences.

During 2011 I re-crafted the website, named it Motorhome Lifers and modernised it with a blog. The early newsletters have been preserved in the trip archive. I reviewed them recently and realised that I haven't included much detail. I think this was because I didn't want to bore my readers, but that I also was trying to avoid sounding as though I was gloating because I was achieving my ambition to travel at such a young age.

My attempts at staying in touch haven't replaced the need to see my closest friends regularly. I have learned to live with the fact that I get to see them in bursts of social activity when we return. I always make a beeline for them as soon as we hit UK soil because face to face conversation can't be beaten. Although we pick up from exactly where we left off as we take the first sips of our drinks, I still find that I miss them when I'm away.

This way of life has given us the opportunity to meet lots of people, and some have become close friends. If we're invited by new pals to go and visit them at their home on a future date, we take them up on the offer wherever possible.

Guidebooks sometimes offer to give an experience equal to having a local show you round, but to have a real person share their community is a privilege and offers invaluable insight into their lives and issues. The genuine kindness and hospitality shown by our hosts helps us get to the heart of where they're from.

When we communicate with people from other countries I have to confess that Mike and I are not proficient in any languages. We spend a lot of time in Spain and took some lessons, however none of it stuck.

I speak appalling school girl French and have recently changed my approach when I interact with French people. I now warn them (in French) that I can't speak their language and apologise, before attempting to converse. This seems to prepare them for the worst as since I started this new strategy individuals seem to have become more tolerant.

Mike is a brilliant non-verbal communicator and uses gestures and facial expressions to convey his meaning. When we were in Belarus he managed to get the full story of a wrecked BMW in a car park from the security guard. Not a single word in any language, let alone Russian, was exchanged - all mimes and gesticulations from both parties.

Mobile phones

We always purchase unlocked mobile phones, usually second hand or reconditioned. This means that we can put any SIM card into the phone, wherever we are and choose the most cost effective deal. We use Giffgaff SIM cards while we're in the UK.

If you have a UK mobile phone, locked, unlocked, on contract, or pay-as-you-go, roaming charges in Europe are high for calls, texts and data. Even if the odd text message is now less than 10p, it soon adds up.

Do the research before leaving home and make sure you know how to switch data services off on your phone before arriving on foreign soil because the charges can be punishing.

Wi-Fi

Wi-Fi is widely available - bars, cafés, restaurants, campsites and in local communities. You can often pick up a signal from outside a bar or café and continue to use the internet without going in. If you need it consistently, perhaps for work, you couldn't rely on this method.

We try not to pay for Wi-Fi, if at all possible, and the spend on drinks and snacks can add up in a restaurant while you're using the service provided.

We recently joined the Fon network by purchasing a modem the company has christened a Fonera. In a nutshell, buying one of these gives access to thousands of Wi-Fi hotspots in several European countries but to get the full in depth information you need to look at the Fon website. It sounded great, which is why we bought one, but having tried it out over the summer of 2014 we have found some drawbacks.

Mike found it impossible to access any Fon spots in France. As you're aware, he finds the technical side of life challenging but this was a real issue, not ineptitude.

I managed to get on line with a Fon hotspot using my phone in Germany but we couldn't use it because I was standing on the pavement in a residential street when a lady came out of her house to ask if I was OK. She thought I was loitering and up to no good. As a result of this we drove to a few addresses that had Fon spots and the signal was too weak to be useable, or there was no suitable parking for the motorhome.

Fon may come into its own in the future but the jury is still out because of our initial glitches.

It doesn't pay to be shy, and a little eccentricity goes a long way, when it comes to finding a free Wi-Fi opportunity. I once unpacked my overnight bag in a packed city centre pub, to retrieve the laptop from the bottom. As I piled the contents on the table and chairs, I noticed the other customers were staring at me. What I class as a normal part of travelling had clearly roused their curiosity.

Mobile phone networks now provide a broadband service which can be accessed to enable you to use the internet, all good options for use in a motorhome, particularly if you're on a field in the middle of nowhere with no Wi-Fi for miles around.

There are 3 ways to do this:

- With a dongle that you plug in to a USB port on a computer.

- A wireless router, known as a Mi-Fi acts as a mobile Wi-Fi hotspot. Some mobile phones can be set up as a mobile hotspot. (See next point below.)

- Tethering is accessing the internet through your mobile phone's connection with any other device. Traditionally, this was accomplished either over USB or Bluetooth. Today, however, the most popular mechanism for accomplishing this is the mobile hotspot. The hotspot on your phone emulates a Wi-Fi router (like the Mi-Fi) so your other devices will connect to it just like they would at home. Some data plans won't allow this because usage shoots up, so double check that this is permitted.

You can get pay as you go, or monthly subscription packages for data. The cost of roaming abroad remains expensive.

Using the Internet to Make Phone Calls

If we have Wi-Fi we use Skype to call home. Skype to Skype calls and texts are free and we have credit on our account for calling landlines. Setting this up is painless, but you need to make sure that your 'co-Skypers' at home know how it all works before you leave. Switching off video at both ends seems to improve call quality for speech.

This summer I tried Viber for voice calls and messages using an 'app.' on my phone. This seems to provide better quality using a mobile broadband signal when no Wi-Fi is available. If you are outside the UK you would need a roaming data package to do this. Viber works on most platforms but not many of my friends have it and so this limits its usefulness for me.

Some of our contacts have WhatsApp. This is another useful free messaging facility that uses data or Wi-Fi rather than an SMS text allowance.

We also use Facebook instant messaging and BlackBerry Messenger. BlackBerry supports video and voice calls for free using Wi-Fi on Android, iPhone and Windows Phone so you don't have to have a BlackBerry to use this service.

I have gone ahead and downloaded these apps as my friends have told me their preferred choice. This has meant I can keep in touch with more of them as not everyone uses the same service.

Phone Cards

Many countries have scrapped phone cards and even payphones, because mobile phone use is so prevalent, but you may get lucky. Find a newsagent and see if they sell phone cards. You need the type where you scratch off an account number on the back and that has a free phone number to access the service. This means that you can dial out from a payphone or a landline.

We found one in Portugal during the winter of 2013/14, which cost €5. International calls cost one cent a minute, and there was no connection fee.

New Friends

When we first started out, if we saw another motorhome coming in the opposite direction, we would wave at each other as if we belonged to a special club. I have noticed this doesn't happen as much these days, perhaps this is because there are so many more motorhomes on the road. The fact that the numbers have gone up shouldn't mean that it becomes less friendly. Try and think of yourself as being a fellow member of a community of like-minded people. Don't be hostile towards other owners and don't forget no-one owns a view, so if someone comes and parks right in front of you and blots out your landscape there's nothing you can do about it. Try not to become territorial, learn to share, and if somewhere gets too crowded you can always move on. That's what the freedom of a motorhome is all about.

During the winter of 2013 we parked next to a day van that a young Spanish man was living in. Although he was near Girona he was from Zaragoza and had driven around the whole country trying to find work. His efforts had been unrewarded and he was sceptical of his chances. I encouraged him to keep trying and not to become despondent.

A couple of months later I received a heartfelt thank you in an email. My optimistic words had boosted his morale and he'd ended up with a good job working on trucks in Germany, even though he didn't speak a word in German when he first started working for the company.

I include this short anecdote because it serves to remind me that as we go about our daily lives we cannot imagine what effect our words or actions are having on the recipient. This example was of a positive reaction but negative words can have a detrimental effect on travellers if they are on their own for long periods of time and not interacting with their peers or people that know them well.

When we arrive somewhere new, Mike jumps out of the van, stretches his back and then gets talking to others. It's a great way to find out local news, views and gossip, enriching the overall experience. It's also important to find out any dangers or annoyances that others may be aware of.

As for me, I don't need to pair up for a double act and so I hang back in the van, unpack, put the kettle on and enjoy a few minutes of peace.

Chapter Eight
Further Afield

While we were away on our first trip Mike read an article written by a couple who had shipped their UK registered motorhome to the USA. This inspired him to do the same and we used it to help us plan. There were three broad categories for us to think about:

- Personal considerations.
- The motorhome.
- What could go wrong?

Personal Considerations

Under this heading I'm covering family issues first, then the legal side.

We had to think about our folks back home. During our first year in Europe, keeping up with friends and family hadn't posed much of a problem, where the distances involved are much shorter. But how would we feel if something serious happened to any of our close family and we were in America? We might have wanted to, but could we afford to return for a life threatening illness or funeral?

As for the legalities, we knew that a British tourist can stay for up to three months without a visa, thanks to the visa waiver programme. However, in order to stay longer we required a B2 visitor visa. We completed the application while we were in the UK and once this had been approved we were interviewed in person at the American Embassy in London. This type of visa is valid for ten years and gives a stay of up to six months at a time. When the six months expired we were supposed to return to our country of residence (i.e. the UK) and not hop across a border to Mexico or Canada to 'reload' it a few days before expiry.

Homeland Security are most worried about non US Citizens living in an RV and working illegally so you need to be able to prove that you have sufficient means to live without employment when you apply.

The piece in the magazine mentioned organisations in the states for RV owners. I had a look at the Family Motor Coach Association (FMCA) website and liked what I read. They provided lots of support for full-timers including insurance, Post Restante service and phone card.

The Motorhome

No matter how much research we did before departure there was no way of knowing how the authorities would interpret the rules when we arrived.

A customs officer has the power to refuse a vehicle entry for any reason and if this occurs you have to foot the bill to ship the motorhome, and meet all the associated costs back to the port of origin.

We chose Charleston in South Carolina and didn't want to formally import our vehicle. A full importation would have meant registration with South Carolina number plates and so we chose a Temporary Import Bond. This allowed us to go anywhere in America for 12 months; however, a day over and she would have been impounded.

The van needed a couple of modifications; a transformer as she was built to take a 220-240v mains electricity supply and the American mains voltage is 110v. We had new gas cylinders (for LPG) installed and this set us back $800 in 2003.

Soon after we arrived we decided not to get the transformer fitted and chose to rely on our solar panel. It had provided us with enough power for a full year in Europe and so we had no reason to suppose that it wouldn't be sufficient for the US trip.

What Could Go Wrong?

What would we do if we had a puncture or needed a new windscreen? European tyre sizes were not available, nor a windscreen. These would have to be shipped from the UK if required, and doing this sounded expensive. The ultimate disaster would be if we had an accident and the van had to be written off. Could we afford that eventuality? We did get four punctures in total and were extremely fortunate that they could be repaired.

The van would require a service and as Fiat didn't have a presence in North America at the time, this could have proved problematic. To cover this we packed what we would need for a service and found a garage that specialised in European models in California.

To begin our adventure we went on a two week fly drive package holiday to Florida and we arrived with time to spare before the motorhome was due to get to the port. The package provided return flights just in case we needed them, but if all went according to plan we would drop the car off with the rental company and not take the return flight home.

We chose Charleston to ship into because of her mild winter climate and Florida for the plentiful supply of cheap flights from the UK.

Our plans didn't come together as smoothly as we had hoped and I'll share some of our experiences with you now.

The journey north from Florida to Charleston took five days and we treated it like a holiday. When we arrived in Charleston we booked into a motel and Mike contacted the office of the shipping agent there. They assured him that we could trust them implicitly.

The motel was dark and dingy - we both had colds, but it was clean and there was a telephone in the room. On the morning following our arrival, after breakfast, I started to work my way through the phone book listing of vehicle insurance agents. Without insurance we would be unable to drive off the dock, let alone motor around America for a year.

Call after call, excuses piled on top of each other; we weren't American, we didn't have US driving licences, they couldn't understand my accent or we didn't have an address in South Carolina. We wanted to go all over the US and Canada but many of the brokers would only provide cover for South Carolina. We had assumed that America was homogeneous and driving from state to state to state would not pose a problem. I was more than a little worried, the evening was approaching. Had we made a naïve and stupid mistake? Weary now, I had got to 'P' in the phone book and the clear and cheerful voice of Cooper Carter of the Pinckney-Carter Company greeted me. He understood my accent. All he required was that we should pay up front with a credit card and he could secure cover for a year.

As we were now the proud owners of an insurance policy it was time to find out how the van was getting on. The shipping agent suggested Mike go down to the office for a chat. It hadn't crossed their minds to let us know that the van had failed the first inspection. The paperwork had been filled out on our behalf and it was incorrect. The customs official assigned to our case found it unintelligible and had marked the form with angry looking question marks. There was no mention on there about the engine. Our agent hadn't known what type it was so he hadn't filled that section in. The agents were confident our van would pass the second inspection and were adamant that Mike didn't need to attend.

We had become a bit fed up with the dingy confines of the motel, and moved to another, more modern one in Mount Pleasant, north of Charleston. Mike bumped into Cooper Carter and he said that there had been a bag snatch story on the news the night before and it had taken place at our previous motel. He was relieved to learn that we weren't the victims, but this added to my sense of foreboding.

Mike was summoned to the shipping agent's office again, our motorhome failed a second time, engine emissions were in question this time and there was only one more chance. Another failure and the van would be driven onto the next available ship to Southampton, and transported back at our expense.

Others had gone ahead of us, we weren't pioneers, but this had no relevance because they would have had different individuals to deal with. The interpretation of the rules is left to each official. If he, or she, decides that your vehicle doesn't meet the criteria then so be it.

This is the official line on the Border Centre Website; 'Imported motor vehicles are subject to U.S. air pollution control (emission) standards, safety standards, and bumper standards. Most vehicles manufactured abroad that conform to these rules are manufactured and exported expressly for sale in the United States. Foreign made vehicles not manufactured for U.S. exports are unlikely to meet all relevant standards.'

Our Customs Officer appeared to have an autocratic approach to the interpretation of the rules. There was no field on any of the forms to tick, with motorhome, tourist or leisure next to it. To me, it seemed that "NO" would suffice, and he didn't care about the implications for us.

By now I was becoming worried and nervous. The aforementioned 'If it were easy, then everyone would do it' saying popped into my head and I tried to tell myself that everything would work out fine but we couldn't have anticipated the hurdles with form filling.

The third meeting with the customs officer was scheduled for the day our flight was due to return to Florida. I checked out of the motel as Mike attended the meeting.

All the research, the theory that we could import our van could become a mockery if the motorhome was deemed not to be roadworthy.

I was in a dither, should I go to the library, or an internet café, should I stay put at the motel? I sat in the car and tried to read my book and as I was about to drive off I looked in the rear view mirror and there was our motorhome, and Mike was driving it. I nearly burst into tears with relief, we were only hours away from our flight. How had Mike done it?

In the end Mike 'instructed' the official saying that as our van was only a year old it would meet the criteria for US emissions whether he fully understood the EU figures or not. At the end of the day we had been granted visitor visas, surely he could see that all we wanted to do was tour the country? We'd be spending thousands of dollars in the process, who was he to deny us our wishes?

We don't know what made the official change his mind but he acquiesced, stamped the forms and our motorhome finally crossed the threshold. Mike received a terse warning that if our 'veer-hear-cul' was not out of the US by 6th November 2004, it would be impounded by the US Customs and Border Protection Agency and we would NEVER see it again. Yess Siree, Mike understood.

I could never have done it, I'm way too cowardly, and if I get a "no" from someone in authority I accept it because of their elevated status. 'Jobsworths' like him enjoy dealing with people of my type. I make their lives much easier.

My admiration for Mike notched skywards, such gallantry and courage in the face of bureaucracy. Hero, prince and knight in shining armour.

During our first year we had skittered over continental Europe like a pinball between the paddles and stops. When we arrived in America our enthusiasm continued unabated and the only time we stopped longer than three days was because Mike sprained his ankle jogging.

We had the attitude that we were enjoying a lifetime of holidays and thought that we may never have such an opportunity again and so we crammed in as much as we could, usually staying for one night at each place.

If we were getting from A to B we used car parks, Walmart car parks, truck stops and slept outside motels, shopping malls, and restaurants. No restaurant ever turned us down when we asked to stop overnight and we always asked if we could stay before placing our order.

The Walmarts in touristy places or near a campground often had a 'no RV parking' sign prominently displayed. 'No' means no when you see a sign like that but at other locations, if we couldn't see one, we would pop in and ask permission to stay from the duty manager, who would indicate a safe area of the car park.

A resident in Flagstaff, Arizona rang the police after we parked outside her house. When the officials arrived, they were unconcerned, we gave our assurances that we would drive away the following morning.

On another occasion we spent the night on a small car park on Long Island. We were across the road from a Gatsby style residence and wondered who could own such a grand mansion. A police vehicle drove past a couple of times and clearly, we must have fitted in as we were undisturbed all night.

We wild-camped (the Americans call it boondocking) in Santa Monica, Montana, Texas, Alaska, Nebraska, in the Californian desert and round the corner from the Canadian parliament building in Ottawa.

I believe that some Americans also park outside casinos, churches and hospitals, but we didn't.

If we weren't 'on the hoof' we enjoyed staying on the campsites at State Parks, National Parks or County Parks as we preferred these to the commercial ones. We camped near rivers, lakes, forests, by the sea and in the desert. Mike's devotion to our motorhome was clear, as he took photographs with a variety of outstanding backdrops.

Another great facility on many campgrounds, was a fire circle. We haven't seen one of these yet in Europe. Most sites also supplied chopped wood and making up a fire in the evening gave us immense pleasure as we could unwind, chat about our experiences that day and plan where to go next.

There is a picture of us below, that I took using the camera's self-timer. The saying goes, 'A picture is worth a thousand words', and not only am I not finding any words at all right now to describe a fire circle, but I'm also blinking - proof that the camera doesn't lie either. It was taken at Yellowstone National Park in 2004.

Shipping

Vehicles can be shipped using what is called a RORO, (roll on, roll off) service and this is what we used. We were allowed to load our belongings, as well as spares for a service, in the van. They had to be neatly packed away in the cupboards and top box. If this is no longer permitted you would need to factor the cost of replacing your housewares on arrival at the host country.

First Base Freight are based in the UK and deal with motorhome shipping. We didn't use this company when we went, but they have a lot of information for motorhomes on their website, if this is something that would interest you.

Another company that organises tours as well as shipping is Seabridge, based in Germany. Although we have never used them, we have spoken to representatives and made contact by email. They organise all shipping, insurance and paperwork.

Insurance

As you know, for our second tour of the States we purchased a motorhome in Florida. We found out that we could save money on the insurance premium by taking US driving tests. However the company contacted us after we had paid up front for the year and told us we owed them more money.

Drive the Americas has a website that provides useful information for more adventurous driving explorations.

Russia and Belarus

In 2012 we took a trip to St Petersburg, via Poland and Belarus. We went with our friends, Jon and Linda, who were in their motorhome. It was a memorable trip and great to go somewhere completely different.

We used a company called Real Russia to obtain our visas for Russia and Belarus.

There are many types of visa for Russia, some involve receiving an invite from a Russian citizen or business. Real Russia handled all this efficiently on our behalf. They were helpful and professional - no question appeared to be too trivial.

In Belarus and Russia the road signs were in Cyrillic and as navigator I tried to learn the shapes of the letters for the destinations we wanted. However, this was easier said than done.

Moscow – **Москва**

Saint Petersburg – **Санкт-Петербург**

My favourite letter looks like a six legged insect – **Ж** .

There was a brand new stretch of road approaching St. Petersburg and I managed to take a quick snap of this road sign, pictured below. At the time I couldn't work out what it meant, although, looking at it now, I think that's airport terminals one and two on the left.

When it came to driving standards the Russians appeared to be in a league of their own, separate from the rest of the world. If Portuguese driving is careless, Greek would be suicidal, and Russian murderous and maniacal.

The main arterial routes are known as 'M' roads, and we took one to St. Petersburg. We saw all types of vehicle on this road; some high end, fast sports cars which were driven as though they were competing in a computer race game.

The roads were greasy when wet and there were ruts in the tarmac. The service vehicles were mostly elderly, (original 1970's design or older) and many others unfit for the road, with bald tyres etc. There is a photo of an elderly emergency vehicle below. I wondered if it could still be in service as an ambulance.

There were only a handful of other vehicles on the road to Novgorod from Pskov but it was only a wide sandy track with chunks of asphalt remaining between crater-like potholes, as you can see in the photo overleaf.

We had heard anecdotes of violence, gun crime and police corruption, but we weren't troubled by this at all in Russia or Belarus.

The Russians have screen mounted cameras to record incidents on the road which is why there are so many harrowing films of Russian road traffic accidents on You Tube.

Driving in Belarus was different to Russia because the roads were almost perfect. There wasn't much traffic, apart from around Minsk where there were more motorists, whose driving was erratic. The condition of the road deteriorated here too. We try to avoid driving at night anywhere we go, but this was particularly important in Belarus because there were horses and carts on the road and they didn't have lights.

We bought insurance at the Belarus border which covered us for both countries. It was inexpensive and third party only.

We stayed overnight in truck stops (TIR Parks), secure hotel car parks and UNESCO sites after closing time. There is a Stellplatz near St Petersburg in the grounds of the conference centre.

Communication

It was impossible to understand anything written in Russian, but we did meet a few people that could speak English. They were shy initially and so for making ourselves understood we generally relied on Mike's mime and gesticulation skills to convey what we wanted.

Jon and Linda had had a few lessons in Russian for a previous visit and remembered some useful phrases. One of them included the word for an English person. To me, this sounded like 'Angler-Chenka'.

One evening, we were desperately hungry and fancied a pizza. Luckily we found a pizzeria in town, but the waiter emphatically denied the existence of an available table. Suddenly, Jon clapped his hands together and as he did this, threw himself on his knees and made an impassioned plea, as if he was praying for his meal. As he did this he cried out "Angler-chenka, angler-chenka".

This transformed our evening as suddenly the Maître d' spoke excellent English and apologised that the only remaining table was situated directly beneath the air conditioning unit.

Tours

Going on an organised tour with other motorhome owners is great fun because you're in a group with like-minded people.

If you don't like an itinerary or being told what time to be up and ready to leave, then this may not be suitable.

If you like the look of a country but are concerned about safety and security then remember that if it was unduly dangerous the tour company wouldn't go there.

Travelling this way is more expensive than if you arranged it all yourself but, clearly, a lot less hassle, because insurance, ferries (or shipping) are arranged on your behalf as well as deciphering the bureaucratic forms.

The Motorhome

Where is Home?

We're sometimes asked where we call home. We both settled in Norfolk in the late 1980's and although we're not native speakers this is where we have planted roots. When we return to the UK we travel the length and breadth of the country as we have family in London, East Yorkshire and Gloucestershire and friends all over the map. We usually base ourselves in Norfolk, not only to catch up with friends, but also to organise routine appointments for ourselves and the van.

The campsite we use is in Mid Norfolk. We are always given a genuine and warm welcome by David, Heather and the family, even though we usually give them virtually no notice of our impending arrival. David's entertaining anecdotes give unrivalled insight into village life. He once took us up onto the church roof. I was proud to have made the ascent and felt honoured that he asked us. The views from the top were stupendous and well worth the close call with spiders' webs, hatchways and narrow step ladders to get there.

Conclusion

While we were away on one of our trips a couple of years ago, I started to feel as though my life lacked meaning. No children. No legacy. Life in the van is always busy but it was all starting to feel like a tired buffet rather than the exciting smorgasbord it had done in previous years.

I read a fascinating book called 'How to Be Idle' by Tom Hodgkinson and this helped me to understand that I wasn't wasting my time. It made me realise that, in fact, our lifestyle had given me time to explore and acquire knowledge about subjects I am interested in. I wouldn't have had the energy or inclination to do this had I been working full time.

Around the time I read the Tom Hodgkinson book I was also recommended a couple more. These were 'Momma and The Meaning of Life' by Irvin D. Yalom and 'Authentic Happiness' by Martin Seligman.

If I had been suffering from a physical complaint a medical doctor would have described me as 'worried well' and although I had absolutely nothing to worry about in life, I felt it lacked direction. It seemed that both these books had been written with someone like me in mind. Through reading these, I realised that I needed to stretch my grey matter beyond the blog, website and writing the occasional magazine article.

It wasn't long before I decided to knuckle down and write a book. My plan was to jot one down about our travels and submit it for publication in the traditional way.

I found it increasingly difficult to get meaningful chunks of the new project under way and my frustration manifested itself in having a short fuse with Mike. My attitude in life can only be described as laid back and easy going so we were both shocked by this personality change and concluded that I must have been having a mid-life crisis.

After much soul searching I decided to ask Mike for a break and some time on my own in order to get 'the book' done. This resulted in us renting a flat in Norwich and enabled me to get on and write. The irony of this being, that in order to create a book about living in a motorhome full-time, I required a flat. This wasn't a 100% necessity; you really do have a home on wheels in a motorhome, but I knew that if I had a stable base it would increase the likelihood of me getting it finished.

As I embraced my new enterprise I learnt about the brave new world of self-publishing and decided that this had to be a better way for me to achieve my goals. I wouldn't have to face rejection by a traditional publisher who didn't think my work was commercially viable. After all, I wanted to create a piece of work, not become the next global icon in the published word.

My first book is available as an e-book and called '*Motorhome Life... A Few Tips and Ideas*' and the first big learning point from this was not to rush – get it proof read first. A friend contacted me soon after she read it to explain that she nearly 'wet herself' laughing because I had inadvertently written that I 'wet myself in the shower'. Of course, what I had meant, was that I covered myself in water from the shower. I removed this howler, ironed out some other creases and published the second edition in September 2014.

While I was working on improving the second edition I was contacted by readers who said they liked the pictures and anecdotes. I decided to overhaul the complete manuscript, included more anecdotes in response to the requests. I also included more factual information.

Having thought initially that I could 'jot' down a book, I haven't yet finished the original one I intended to write. I will get it done, but right now, I'm off to get a glass of water, an aspirin and have a lie down. 'Jotting down' a book? What was I thinking?

Please use the website to see where we are and what we're up to. If you would like to ask anything about our lifestyle you can contact us. If there is a reason why I can't get back to you within 48 hrs, I will have updated the website to let you know why.

Happy travels, Ali Kingston

November 2014

####

Thank you for reading my book. If you enjoyed it, please take a moment to leave me a review at your favourite retailer.

Thanks!

Keep in Touch With Ali

Check the website www.motorhomelifers.co.uk for updates;
or choose your favourite way to follow:

Twitter: https://twitter.com/motorhomelifer

Facebook: https://www.facebook.com/Motorhomelifers

Pinterest: http://pinterest.com/motorhomelifers

LinkedIn: http://www.linkedin.com/in/motorhomelifer

Google Plus: https://plus.google.com/+AliKingston/posts

Phew - I think that covers it

The Motorhome

Web Links

I have typed out the URL for you to enter into a browser, or you could use a search engine.

AA Touring Tips Country By Country – http://bit.ly/1oICEeT
AA Low Emission Zones (LEZ) – http://bit.ly/1d6m9Rq
ACSI Camping in Europe – http://bit.ly/1q0Ix45
ADAC - German Automobile Club – http://bit.ly/1rc3ER3
Aires in France Book – http://bit.ly/1rU4u8T
Aria Assistance – http://bit.ly/1OAtWY6

B2 Visitor Visa – http://1.usa.gov/1eFXqnT
Baltic Parking - Stellplatz in St. Petersburg – http://bit.ly/Zmrrrn
Blackberry Messenger – http://bit.ly/1uj21YM
Border Centre Website – http://bit.ly/1qh5jEM
Britstops – http://www.britstops.com/
Buying a Used Motorhome (Out and About Live Publication) – http://bit.ly/1BF1b7U
Buying Your First Motorhome – http://bit.ly/1rbtrZI

Camping and Caravanning Club – http://bit.ly/1lpkYES
Camping-Cars France (For finding Aires) – http://bit.ly/1rc4opA
Car-A-Tow - Tow Frames – http://www.caratow.com/
Caravan Club – http://bit.ly/NXVFva
Contact US – http://www.motorhomelifers.co.uk/contact.html

Defra (taking pets abroad) – http://bit.ly/1sBLQ8u
Drive The Americas – http://bit.ly/ZlSeEl
Düsseldorf Show – http://bit.ly/1vAa3tt

DVLA – http://bit.ly/1bgiumb
DVLA Driving Licence Categories – http://bit.ly/1xG4yxZ

EHIC (European Health Insurance Card) – http://bit.ly/1nNAA7B
Endsleigh – http://bit.ly/1yFgpxw

Facebook Instant Messaging – http://on.fb.me/1l1jHAH
Family Motor Coach Association – http://www.fmca.com/
Fiamma Levelling Ramps – http://bit.ly/1sVCV2I
First Base Freight Motorhome Shipping – http://bit.ly/1rn3zuo
Fon – http://bit.ly/1suooKa
Forest River Berkshire Brochure 2008 – http://bit.ly/1vda2eV
Forest River Sunseeker Brochure 2006 – http://bit.ly/1xtczlk
Furgo VW – http://www.furgovw.org/
France Passion – http://bit.ly/Zhcdnx

Gaslow refillable gas cylinders – http://bit.ly/ZgZm4Q
GB Privilege (Motorhome Tours) – http://bit.ly/1rQh88Q
George Bernard Shaw Quotations – http://bit.ly/1rX5RVM
Giffgaff – http://giffgaff.com/
Giffgaff. Special offer SIM order page – http://bit.ly/ZCv0ty

HelpX – http://www.helpx.net/
Housesitting with Mind My House – http://bit.ly/1yGFIiW

JML – http://bit.ly/1rN0MOy
Justgo Motorhome Hire – http://www.justgo.uk.com/
Lazydays RV – http://www.lazydays.com/
LPG in Spain – http://bit.ly/1tpvuv1
Light Emitting Diode Bulbs (LED) – http://bit.ly/ZcD4RI

MagBaz Travels – http://bit.ly/ZMb8oN

Martin Lewis - Money Saving Expert – http://bit.ly/1fVmQjY

Memory Foam Warehouse – http://bit.ly/1q9DpdQ

Milenco Levelling Ramps – http://bit.ly/1ujIck9

Mobile RV - Parts and Accessories – http://bit.ly/1vEJPpS

Motorhome 365 (Full-Timing Association - Information and Forum) – http://bit.ly/ZMcrnG

Motorhome and Campervan Magazine – http://bit.ly/1vdjRcC

Motorhome and Caravan Show – http://bit.ly/1p9FA3U

Motorhome Facts (Forum and Information) – http://bit.ly/1uro26I

Motorhome Fun (Forum and Information) – http://bit.ly/1ptyJjQ

Motorhome Lifers Blog – http://bit.ly/ZhhviX

Motorcaravan Motorhome Monthly.
Magazine (MMM - Out and About Live) – http://bit.ly/1uuy05t

Out and About Live Forum – http://bit.ly/10Dyehs

Payload (Out and About Live Article) – http://bit.ly/1oItug1

Pegasus Motorhome Finance – http://bit.ly/1pzZSRZ

Pinkney Carter Insurance, South Carolina – http://bit.ly/1rcHoXl

Polarity – http://bit.ly/ZFlM0t

Portugal Camping Car (Search for Aires in Portugal, in Portuguese) – http://bit.ly/1vAoCxb

Practical Motorhome – http://bit.ly/1E4UQXp

Promobil (Stellplatz Search throughout Europe in German) – http://bit.ly/1fHhVA3

Real Russia (Visas and Driving in Russia) – http://bit.ly/1s3i6As

Reimo Door Curtains – http://bit.ly/1xUEI9s

Reimo Mosquito Nets – http://bit.ly/1y0FqSy

RoadPro – http://bit.ly/Z7v306

Romahome – http://bit.ly/1pIHG84
Russia Trip Photographs – http://bit.ly/1q0hCoQ

SC Sporthomes – http://bit.ly/1E4Rtjf
Seabridge – http://bit.ly/1pFnp4c
Search for Sites – http://bit.ly/1uMq9DR
Spartamet bicycles – http://bit.ly/1nSix0H
SvTech – http://bit.ly/1rN0bw0

Temporary Import Bond – http://1.usa.gov/1sY57lB
Thatcham Class 1 Alarm – http://bit.ly/10Auf56
The Motorhome Security Handbook by James Brown –
http://www.motorhomesecurityhandbook.com/?page_id=4
Travel Nation – http://bit.ly/Z3L874

US Energy Information Administration for Data on Fuel Prices –
http://1.usa.gov/1oMXjke

Vayacamping – http://bit.ly/ZmEs4e
Viber – http://www.viber.com/

WhatsApp – http://bit.ly/1knPLNt
Wildax Aurora Spec Table – http://bit.ly/1ptDM3O
Wildax Cutie – http://bit.ly/1uEbYAo
Wildax Motorhomes – http://bit.ly/1oLCUu3
Wildcamping UK – http://www.wildcamping.co.uk/
Which Motorhome Magazine – http://bit.ly/1tkovDJ
Workaway – http://www.workaway.info/

Acknowledgements

There are many people who have helped me by providing advice and words of encouragement with writing, but unfortunately I can't remember you all. If you did - thank you and sorry for my scatty brain.

I'm not too befuddled to remember; Matt Adams, Andy Blizzard, Catherine Blizzard, Liz Davie, Ola Fagbohun, Alison Fair, Katrina Harrison, Paul Hursey, Jon and Linda Reed, Bill and Jackie Payne, Doug Vallgren, Cas Wright.

Thank you. You may have only said a few words but the seeds were sowed and they are finally germinating.

For proof reading; Chris and Maria B, Carmel O' Donohoe, Paul K, Jill and Tom Maguire, Catherine Tranmer.

To Jean Woods for brilliant assistance with editing and grammar as well as straight as a die feedback, with loads of laughter.

To my beta readers; Allison Brown, Jill Glennsansum and Alison Wade.

Thank you to my parents, Robin and Jill Davie for getting me started with my journey on the planet and my induction into the excitement of independent world travel.

Last but not least, to Mike, this book is for you. Your love and support has enabled me to realise my ambitions firstly to travel and then to write. I always dreamt of having someone to share the view with and together we have made this possible. You have the unrivalled ability to endure my mixed messages, and push me out of the procrastination rut, because - let's face it, I'm no different to anyone else on that score.

About the Author

Ali Kingston was born in Lincolnshire in 1965. Her introduction to a life on the move was immediate as her father was in the Royal Air Force. She embraced the cycle of packing, unpacking and repacking as it represented an opportunity to go somewhere new. She went to Badminton School, Bristol, and trained as a Registered General Nurse at The Royal London Hospital. Shortly after qualifying she moved to Norfolk.

A need to explore different career options lead her to work in pharmaceutical sales and to train as a nutritional therapist. Following the publication of her first book, Motorhome Life, A Few Tips and Ideas, Ali would now describe herself as writer and traveller, both of which suit her itinerant nature.

Ali picked Mike up in a bar in Norwich in 2000. She didn't literally pick him up, although that would explain why her shoulder hurts so much these days. Her fate with Mike, as a traveller, was sealed a few weeks later on their package holiday to Gran Canaria. Most men would have dumped the new girlfriend after she ran out of toiletries and underwear but Mike wasn't put off by this debacle and soon she was over stuffing a backpack with clothes she was unlikely to need for her first serious independent backpacking trip to India. For this she learnt the importance of keeping a travel diary from her sister, Catherine.

Globe-trotting in a motorhome meant she had to cope with three in her relationship but, this didn't prevent her from continuing with 'dear diary' jottings.

Expect more publications as the stack of journals is now half her height. She's not overly tall, but half her height is notable, especially when you don't have anywhere to store stuff.

Notes

Use this section to start planning your own trip.

8965255R00079

Printed in Great Britain
by Amazon.co.uk, Ltd.,
Marston Gate.